Virginia Celebrates

Published by Thomasson-Grant, Inc.
Copyright ©1992 by
The Council of the Virginia Museum of Fine Arts.

Text by Rosemary Lanahan

Design by Lisa Lytton-Smith
and Kerry Kuehner Associates
All reproductions from the collection of
the Virginia Museum of Fine Arts
courtesy of the Museum.
Photographs ©1992 by Fred Sons,
unless otherwise credited below.
Cover Photographs: ©1992 by Renée Comet; Page 11: Courtesy of
The Virginia Division of Tourism; Page 14: Joseph Szaszfai;
Page 23: David Milton Browne; Page 29: Leonard G. Phillips;
Page 49: Richmond Times Dispatch; Page 55: Danville Chamber
of Commerce; Page 61: Matt Gentry/Charlottesville Daily Progress;
Page 83 (Woodlawn Plantation): William Bugbee; Page 83
(The Rose Circle): Ross Chapple; Page 91: Courtesy of The Virginia
Museum of Fine Arts; Page 99: Nancy Andrews; Page 125:
Everett C. Johnson; Page 133: William G. McClure; Page 141:
Suzanne Grandis; Page 149: Courtesy of Barter Theatre.

Printed by Progress Printing, Lynchburg, Virginia.

99 98 97 96 95 94 93 92   5 4 3 2 1

Library of Congress Cataloging-in-Publication Data

Virginia celebrates: recipes and ideas for entertaining / the Council of
  the Virginia Museum of Fine Arts.
      p. cm.
  Includes index.
  ISBN 1-56566-015-3 :
  1. Cookery. 2. Festivals--Virginia. I. Virginia Museum of Fine
Arts. Council.
TX714.V56 1992
641.5--dc20   92-13533
                                                  CIP

Thomasson-Grant
One Morton Drive
Charlottesville, Virginia 22903-6806
(804) 977-1780

Virginia Celebrates

Recipes and Ideas for Entertaining

The Council of
the Virginia Museum of Fine Arts

Thomasson-Grant
Charlottesville, Virginia

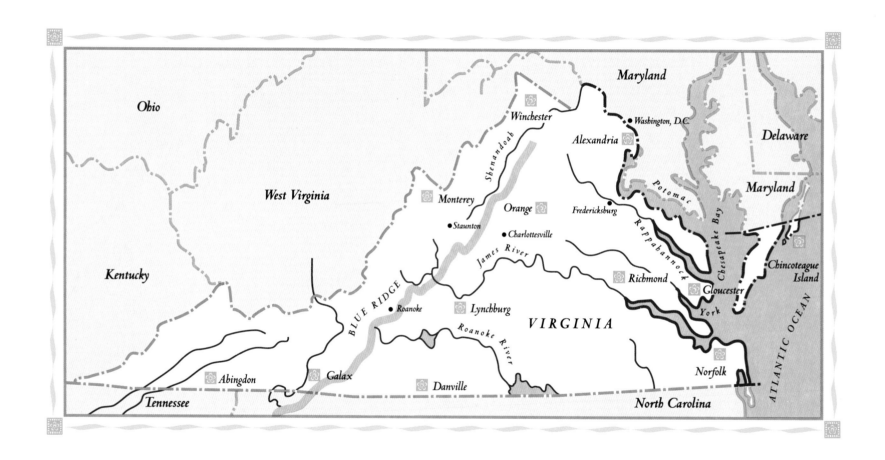

CONTENTS

FOREWORD

Long ago, Virginia was honored with the starring role as our nation's birthplace. In the three centuries since, Virginians have woven into their history a tapestry of cultures and traditions to create an exquisite array of colors and patterns. From the wild drama of the Chincoteague Pony Roundup off Virginia's Eastern Shore and the dreamy sophistication of an after-ballet supper in Richmond to the frosty hues and heady aromas of a springtime maple festival in the Allegheny highlands and the summery bustle and cooling breezes of a brunch beside the James River, Virginia has mastered the art of entertaining.

In these pages, you will also discover that, as the home of America's first statewide visual arts education system, the Virginia Museum of Fine Arts is among the state's proudest possessions. Here we bring you a sampling of the hundreds of paintings, sculptures, and other works of art that inspire thousands of visitors each year to see them in person. As part of that museum's life for nearly four decades, The Council of the Virginia Museum is proudest of all to boast one of the liveliest volunteer art support groups anywhere in America. With this project, for example, the Council has pledged to donate all its proceeds to the Museum's extensive statewide education and outreach program.

As you read and enjoy this unusual book, we promise you a wealth of treasured recipes and colorful, creative ideas. Celebrate Virginia with us through this special sampling of artistic and culinary treasures. We invite you to share the joy of Virginia's greatest social pleasure: serving the finest of foods to bring family and friends closer together.

THE COUNCIL OF
THE VIRGINIA MUSEUM OF FINE ARTS
RICHMOND

INTRODUCTION

Virginia's love affair with food started early and has stayed late. From the time the Indians introduced the first settlers to the possibilities of maize, the bounty of sea and land has been inextricably woven into the fabric of Virginians' lives, not only at the basic level of sustenance, but also as part of their social fabric, their economy, their politics, and their relationship with the soil.

It is not, therefore, surprising that the first cookbook published in America was the work of a Virginia author, Mary Randolph. She was born in 1762 at Tuckahoe Plantation (the locale of some of our menu photographs) and grew up there, etching her initials in a windowpane to preserve her memory. She was related to both Thomas Jefferson and John Marshall, the third chief justice of the Supreme Court, and it is reasonable to assume that they were frequent guests at her table.

Mary Randolph was 62 when *The Virginia Housewife, or Methodical Cook* (1824) was published. She was both a scientific and a precise cook, and as Shirley Abbott writes in her foreword to a 1984 reissue of *The Virginia Housewife*, "She had been the lady of the manor both on a Virginia plantation . . . and in a Richmond town house, and the proprietor of a boarding house besides. She had been deeply involved with her husband in two political scandals that reached into the White House and beyond the Mississippi." (Nothing ever changes!) If she had wanted to write a family saga, Abbott notes, "she would have had more than enough material. But cooking was her lifelong passion. She chose a cookbook rather than a novel to embody her experience – inside kitchens and out of them."

What she ended up chronicling, although the term was not in the 19th-century vocabulary, was a Virginia lifestyle, one of civility, courtesy, and spontaneity, tempered with traditional structure. It is no less so today.

Breakfasts

HIGHLAND MAPLE FESTIVAL
MONTEREY

No community in recorded history has existed without arts and crafts. From the first cave drawings and crude fire pots to Jasper Johns' paintings and Milano furniture, the urge for self-expression finds its outlet. The desire is irrepressible, the expression is accessible to all.

Every March, Highland County, high in the "dark and rumpled Alleghenies," pays homage to this creativity during its Arts and Crafts Festival. And since it's maple-sugaring time, being a practical people, they also celebrate the Maple Festival. Maple sugar and syrup have been produced in this area for more than 200 years, with some trees nearing 300 years old. On the sugar tour, you can appreciate the cost (and the taste) of pure maple syrup. Highland County is also the home of the famous and delectable Allegheny Mountain trout, and you may view thousands at the trout farm, from fingerlings to trophy size.

The arts and crafts are exhibited everywhere in Highland County — on the courthouse lawn in Monterey, in the schools, the firehouse, and the library. Whatever you like, it's here: handwoven baskets, twig furniture, tole ware, quilts, handmade knives, barn signs, oil paintings, watercolors, ceramics. You'll also find every imaginable maple goody, stoneground cornmeal, buckwheat flour, country sausage, and other indigenous delectables.

Held on a weekend, the Highland Maple Festival is a perfect family minivacation. It is also definitely an occasion for rugged clothing. Because of the high elevation and the time of year, the weather can be chilly. Plan to wear warm clothes and boots, especially if you're touring the sugar camps.

The universality of fine craftsmanship in everyday objects is vividly represented in the Virginia Museum collections by a mantel clock (page 13) by Charles F. A. Voysey, the 19th-century architect and designer who was a leader in the English Arts and Crafts Movement. The clock's sheer exuberance bespeaks the delight the artist must have had in making it. He designed this particular clock for his own house. At the time, it was customary to include sayings or mottoes as part of the decorative motif on such objects. Here, a banner on the clock's face carries the motto "Time and Tide Wait for No Man," and instead of numerals, the face has letters forming the Latin words *tempus fugit* (time flies). The body of the clock, painted in bright colors, features a landscape with flowers, trees, and two sailboats in the water. On the top are stylized gilt birds; the upper side panels bear a floral vine motif.

A day at the festival demands stamina — there is so much to see and do. So our prefestival breakfast menus are hearty fare focusing on foods traditional in this area: baked apples and spicy mountain trout or link sausages and buckwheat cakes with Highland maple syrup.

BAKED APPLES
Ginger and apricots make the difference.

Apples
Dried apricots, chopped
Walnuts, chopped
Crystallized ginger, chopped
Butter

❄ Preheat oven to 350°.

❄ Core desired number of apples and peel 1-inch strip from top. Fill with a mixture of apricots, walnuts, and ginger. Dot generously with butter.

❄ Bake uncovered 45 minutes or until tender. Serve warm.

SPICY MOUNTAIN TROUT
An extremely easy fish dish bursting with a medley of flavors

1 large mountain trout, filleted
3 tablespoons maple syrup
2 tablespoons mayonnaise
3 tablespoons whole-grain Dijon mustard
Freshly grated pepper

❄ Wash and dry trout fillets and place on foil-lined pan, skin side down. Pour syrup evenly over fish. Spread with mayonnaise, then mustard. Season with ground pepper to taste.

❄ Broil until crisp and almost blackened, about 10 minutes.

❄ Serves 2

POTATO CRISPS
These are low-cal, low-fat, and better than potato chips.

1 potato per person
Salt
Pepper

❄ Heat oven to 350°.

❄ Scrub potatoes but do not peel. Slice ⅛-inch thin. Lay slices in single layer on greased cookie sheet and place in oven. Bake about 30 to 40 minutes, or until golden brown. Remove from oven and sprinkle with salt and pepper.

CORN LIGHT BREAD

2 cups yellow cornmeal
¾ cup all-purpose flour
1 cup sugar
2 ¾ teaspoons baking powder
¼ teaspoon salt
2 cups buttermilk
1 tablespoon solid shortening

❊ Heat oven to 350°.

❊ Mix cornmeal, flour, sugar, baking powder, and salt. Add buttermilk and blend.

❊ Heat shortening in 9 x 5 x 3-inch loaf pan in oven; when hot and melted, add batter and bake 1 hour.

❊ Makes 1 loaf

BUCKWHEAT CAKES
An old Monterey recipe

1 cup buckwheat flour
½ cup white flour
1 ½ teaspoons baking powder
1 tablespoon brown sugar
1 teaspoon salt
1 tablespoon soft shortening or
   vegetable oil
1 ½ cup milk
1 egg

❊ Mix flours, baking powder, sugar, and salt. Add shortening, milk, and egg. Stir until batter is slightly lumpy. Pour small portions of batter onto a lightly greased hot griddle and cook until bubbles appear. Turn cakes only once.

❊ Recipe can be doubled or tripled. Serve with Highland maple syrup or maple butter.

❊ Makes 6 to 8 6-inch pancakes

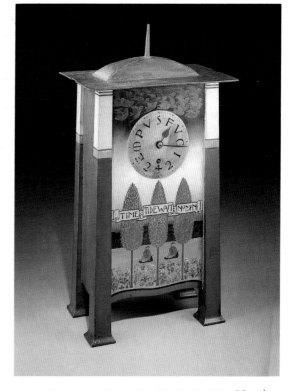

Charles F. Annesley Voysey (English, 1857-1941), *Mantel Clock*, 1896, painted wood, brass, clockworks. Collection of the Virginia Museum of Fine Arts, Richmond. Gift of Sydney and Frances Lewis.

John Frederick Herring (English, 1795-1865), *Hunting Scenes: Streaming Off*, ca. 1840, oil on
canvas. Collection of the Virginia Museum of Fine Arts, Richmond. The Paul Mellon Collection.

THE HUNT BREAKFAST

MENU

Hot Tomato Bouillon

Quail *with* Port Sauce *on* Wild Rice

Scalloped Oysters

Acorn Squash Rings
with Spinach

Warm Fruit Compote

Smithfield Ham

Sweet Potato Biscuits

Platter *of* Sweet Treats
including
Mini Chocolate Cakes
Oatmeal Tarts
Wee Lemon Cakes

*F*ox hunting became a recognized sport in England some time in the 1600s, and true to the British predilection for sport, it quickly became very popular. After a hearty breakfast to fortify themselves against the chill of an English dawn, hunters ravenous for food and drink came home at the end of the day to an equally hearty hunt supper.

There is evidence that fox hunting of sorts came to the American colonies at about the same time, with the arrival of one Robert Brooke, who traveled here from England in his own private ship, accompanied by his family, 28 servants, and a pack of hounds. He is officially designated as the first Master of Hounds in colonial America. The sport spread rapidly from one region to another, probably because the rules of the game were a good deal more relaxed and less structured than in England. Both Washington and Jefferson were avid fox hunters. According to his diaries, General Washington often managed a few hours of hunting between Revolutionary battles. Apparently even Martha hunted occasionally.

The craze for the sport grew steadily over the years until it was curtailed by the Civil War, after which only two hunt clubs survived in the United States. By the 1960s, the sport had been revived, and there were 90 recognized hunt clubs. Now rapid urbanization is fast eroding both the countryside and the natural habitat of the fox.

Sideboard, probably from the Shenandoah Valley of Virginia, 1790-1800, mahogany, satinwood inlay. Collection of the Virginia Museum of Fine Arts, Richmond. Gift of Mrs. Richard S. Reynolds, Jr., in memory of her son, J. Sargeant Reynolds.

The Paul Mellon Collection of British Sporting Paintings in the Virginia Museum contains countless depictions of the fox hunt, but none captures the mood, the movement, and the exhilaration of the chase better than John Frederick Herring's *Streaming Off*. The hounds, in full cry, scurry over the hill, brilliant coats flash against the lowering sky, and horses leap over fences. It is a painting to which, as the French novelist François Mauriac so aptly put it, "the eye listens." Its excitement is almost palpable. *Streaming Off* was chosen as the focal point of our traditional hunt breakfast, along with another fine example of art, an American sideboard from the Virginia Museum collection (previous page). Like the food they enhance, these two pieces combine the best of our English and American heritage. The photograph opposite includes a collection of antique stirrup cups, which traditionally held the prehunt drink riders consumed before they rode off.

Perhaps because of the American penchant for getting on with things, the traditional English hunt supper evolved in this country into the hunt breakfast. We can only imagine what foods comprised those very first repasts. Traditionally, though, they were not for the faint-hearted or the delicate appetite. Even today they are lavish, hearty, and bounteous. (Those who want a culinary challenge can attempt to come up with a low-calorie version!) The menu reflects the blessings of our land: scalloped oysters, quail on wild rice, a compote of warm fruit, Smithfield ham and sweet potato biscuits, a platter of sweet treats. You may wish to introduce regional dishes into your own menu: a Cajun dish from the bayou, red flannel hash from New England, a Tex-Mex casserole from the Southwest, Dungeness crab from the Northwest.

But *do* have a hunt breakfast. It is a gracious, imaginative, and easy way to entertain, as most of the dishes can be prepared in advance. And you don't have to have a fox hunt afterward. Your guests will still enjoy the food and the perpetuation of a sporting tradition, and the fox will be eternally grateful!

HOT TOMATO BOUILLON

3 cups chicken or beef broth
1 cup coarsely chopped onion
1 coarsely chopped rib of celery
½ cup coarsely chopped green pepper
2 teaspoons dark brown sugar
2 tablespoons cider vinegar
1 stick cinnamon
6 to 8 whole cloves
1 teaspoon salt
1 tablespoon butter
1 bay leaf
4 to 5 whole allspice or
   ¼ teaspoon ground
3 ½ cups tomato juice

Combine broth, onion, celery, green pepper, brown sugar, vinegar, cinnamon, cloves, salt, butter, bay leaf, and allspice in large saucepan and simmer ½ hour. Strain and add tomato juice. Reheat and serve very hot in mugs.

Makes 8 ¾-cup servings

QUAIL WITH PORT SAUCE

12 quail, cleaned, rinsed, and dried
Salt and pepper
12 pieces onion, small enough for
   each bird cavity
12 pieces cored apple, small enough
   for each bird cavity
Butter, softened for rubbing
12 strips raw bacon

Port sauce:
   1 tablespoon minced scallions
   1 tablespoon drippings from roasting pan
      (add more butter if needed)
   1 ½ cups beef stock
   ¼ to ½ cup port wine
   Fresh sprigs rosemary, tarragon,
      or Italian parsley for garnish

Preheat oven to 400°.

Season cavities with salt and pepper. Add chunk of onion and apple to each cavity. Rub outside of each bird with butter. Wrap bacon around each bird and place birds breast side up in roasting pan. Bake 30 to 40 minutes, covered with foil.

Remove foil, discard bacon, and brown breasts under broiler. Remove from broiler and keep warm. Do not overcook.

To make port sauce, sauté scallions in drippings. Add beef stock and port. Boil to reduce to about 1 cup.

Correct seasonings and spoon over birds on beds of wild rice. Garnish with fresh sprigs of rosemary, tarragon, or Italian parsley.

Serves 6

SCALLOPED OYSTERS

3 cups finely crumbled no-fat saltine
   crackers
1 ½ quarts oysters
Salt
Pepper
Nutmeg
Seafood seasoning
6 tablespoons melted butter
¾ cup milk or cream

Preheat oven to 350°.

Grease a shallow 9 x 12-inch baking dish and
cover bottom with a layer of cracker crumbs.

Layer oysters, seasonings and remaining
crumbs mixed with melted butter ending with
crumbs and seasoning. Dribble each layer with a
little milk and pour remaining milk over top
layer.

Cover and refrigerate. May be prepared ahead
of time.

Bake uncovered 40 minutes, or until lightly
browned and bubbling.

Serves 8

ACORN SQUASH RINGS WITH SPINACH

Pine nuts add crunch and flavor.

2 medium acorn squash
1 tablespoon lemon juice
Ground ginger
Salt and pepper

Preheat oven to 350°. Parboil squash 10 minutes to soften enough to slice. Cut 3 ¾ inch
slices from each squash. Remove seeds. Place
rings in ovenproof dish with lemon juice and
enough water to cover bottom of dish. Sprinkle
with ginger, salt, and pepper. Bake until rings are
barely tender.

2 packages frozen chopped spinach
3 tablespoons pine nuts
6 tablespoons butter, divided
2 tablespoons flour
2 tablespoons minced onion
½ teaspoon freshly ground nutmeg
1 teaspoon Worcestershire sauce

Cook spinach according to package directions,
then drain well, reserving liquid. In 2 tablespoons butter, sauté pine nuts until lightly
browned: set aside. Melt remaining butter and
saute onion until limp. Add flour and ½ cup
spinach liquid. Cook until thickened. Add
spinach, nutmeg, and pine nuts. Mound spinach
mixture on squash slices and heat in oven about
20 minutes. May be prepared ahead and refrigerated. Allow additional reheating time if cold.

Serves 6

WARM FRUIT COMPOTE

1 20-ounce can peach halves
1 20-ounce can apricot halves
1 20-ounce can pineapple wedges
1 20-ounce can plums
2 cups fresh cranberries, poached in
   sugar and water
¼ cup melted butter
½ cup brown sugar
2 teaspoons curry powder
Fresh mint for garnish

Preheat oven to 325°.

Drain peaches, apricots, pineapple, plums,
and cranberries. Place in 3-quart baking dish.
Mix butter, sugar, and curry powder and pour
over fruit.

Bake 1 hour or cook on top of stove. Better if
made a day ahead of serving time and reheated.

Garnish with fresh mint.

Serves 16 to 20

SMITHFIELD HAM

12- to 14-pound Smithfield ham
7 cups water
Ground cloves
Honey
Fine cracker crumbs
Whole cloves (optional)

Soak ham in cold water to cover 12 to 24 hours.

Remove ham from water and scrub well with a brush to remove all coating.

Preheat oven to 500°. Put ham in roaster, fat side up, with 7 cups of water. Cover tightly. Let temperature come back to 500° and cook ham at this temperature for 15 minutes.

Turn off oven. DO NOT OPEN DOOR.

Three hours later, turn oven on 500°, and when the temperature registers 500°, start timing and cook for 20 minutes. Turn oven off. DO NOT OPEN THE OVEN DOOR. After 3 hours, ham is done.

When ham is cool enough to handle, remove skin. Cut gashes in fat on the diagonal to make a diamond pattern. Sprinkle with ground cloves, smear with honey, and sprinkle with fine cracker crumbs. Put whole cloves in center of diamonds, if desired. Another good topping is a mixture of mustard and brown sugar smeared over the fat.

Bake at 250° until top of ham is golden, crispy, and crunchy, about 20 to 30 minutes. Your ham will be tender and moist, not dry, as is so often the case. Slice very thin.

SWEET POTATO BISCUITS

2 cups flour
4 teaspoons baking powder
½ teaspoon salt
1 tablespoon brown sugar, packed
⅛ teaspoon cinnamon
⅛ teaspoon nutmeg
½ stick butter
¼ cup shortening
⅓ cup finely chopped pecans
⅔ cup cooked, mashed sweet potatoes
½ cup half-and-half

Preheat oven to 425°.

Sift flour, baking powder, salt, brown sugar, cinnamon, and nutmeg into a medium-sized bowl.

Cut in butter and shortening until mixture is mealy. Add pecans and stir. Mix potatoes and half-and-half, and add to flour mixture.

Knead briefly on a floured surface. Roll out to ½-inch thickness, cut with a round cutter.

Place on greased baking sheet and bake for 12 to 15 minutes.

Makes 18 biscuits

MINI CHOCOLATE CAKES

4 4-ounce squares unsweetened chocolate
2 sticks margarine
I cup chopped pecans
I ¾ cups sugar
I cup all-purpose flour
4 eggs, beaten
I teaspoon vanilla

⬚ Preheat oven to 350°.

⬚ Melt chocolate and margarine over low heat in heavy saucepan. Remove from heat and add pecans, stirring to coat.

⬚ Combine sugar, flour, eggs, and vanilla. Mix only to blend. Combine both mixtures, stirring carefully.

⬚ Line small muffin pans with mini paper liners. Fill almost full, as the cakes do not rise very much.

⬚ Bake about 20 minutes.

⬚ Makes 6 dozen

OATMEAL TARTS

2 sticks butter, melted
I cup packed dark brown sugar
I cup packed light brown sugar
4 cups old-fashioned oatmeal
¾ teaspoon salt
I tablespoon vanilla
¾ cup chopped pecans

⬚ Preheat oven to 350°.

⬚ Melt butter. Add sugars, oatmeal, salt, vanilla, pecans and mix well.

⬚ Fill miniature muffin pans ¾ full. Bake 12 to 15 minutes. Remove from oven. While hot, using a spoon, push mixture which has baked out over the edge back into the pan, making the tart compact. Cool 10 minutes before removing from pan.

⬚ Yields 72

WEE LEMON CAKES

I cup butter
2 cups sugar
4 eggs, well beaten
3 cups flour
2 teaspoons baking powder
I scant cup milk
I teaspoon vanilla
Grated rind and juice of I lemon
Grated rind and juice of I orange
2 ¾ cups powdered sugar

⬚ Preheat oven to 350°.

⬚ Cream butter and sugar and add eggs. Sift together flour and baking powder. Add flour mixture and milk alternately to butter mixture. Add vanilla and mix well.

⬚ Drop cake batter by teaspoons into greased and floured small muffin tins. Bake for 10 minutes. Remove from muffin tins.

⬚ Strain lemon and orange juices and add rinds to juices. Stir in powdered sugar and mix thoroughly.

⬚ Using kitchen tongs, dip each cake into juice mixture and place on a wire rack with wax paper underneath to catch the drippings.

⬚ Serve warm or cold. Freezes well.

⬚ Makes 4 dozen

Brunches

James River Batteau Festival
LYNCHBURG

Menus

Peach Smoothie

Custard French Toast *with* Orange Butter

Bacon Curls

Coffee

Sliced Cantaloupe, Blueberries,
and Strawberries *in* Apricot Nectar

Garden-fresh Frittata Garnished *with*
Blanched Snow Peas *and* Cherry Tomatoes

Potato Corn Muffins

Sticky Roll-ups

Iced Coffee, Lynchburg Style

"*I*nstant Tradition." It may seem a contradiction in terms, but that's what the James River Batteau Festival has become in the few years since its inception. And its scope of activities, along with its attendance, keeps growing every year.

The idea for the festival was spawned in 1983 when power shovels at a construction site in Richmond unearthed portions of some old batteaux, the 18th-century supply boats used to haul cargo up and down the James River from the port of supply to outposts and burgeoning towns in the wilderness. Before there were railroads, airplanes, or superhighways, the river bore the merchant boats to the frontier, transporting necessary goods and an occasional luxury item, riding the first wave of an era of economic prosperity.

Built by volunteers, the batteaux used in the festival are authentic replicas of the originals. The festival's founder, Joe Ayers, rhapsodizes about the beauty of the batteau. "It's very much a work of art, a finely sculpted piece of wood. And when you put it in the river, with its canopy of sycamores and oaks, then you're standing in a painting." The men and women who pole the river find the batteau a test of both strength and skill, a vehicle that allows them to relive the romance and history of a time long past.

The festival starts each June in Lynchburg, a beautiful river city cupped in the foothills of the Blue Ridge Mountains. The boats are launched one day and poled away the next afternoon, the beginning of an eight-day journey punctuated by stops in historic towns along the 200-year-old route. Each evening, they are greeted by enthusiastic crowds, and the cultural heritage of the river is celebrated in dance, homegrown music, and hearty Virginia cooking.

The lure and life-sustaining quality of the river is as old as man himself. From the Egyptian collection of the Virginia Museum comes a Twelfth Dynasty boat model (next page) from a tomb at El Bersheh, showing servants rowing their master into his second existence. The contents of the tombs closely reflected Egyptian life through objects made with great sophistication and beauty. There is an amazing similarity between these boatmen and the crews of the batteaux. The romance of the river is indeed timeless, whether it be the Nile or the James!

We begin our eight-day batteau festivities with a brunch served before our early-afternoon trek to the riverbank to wish the batteaux "bon voyage." An easily assembled meal featuring some traditional Virginia dishes, it appeals to both adults and children — this after all is a family affair. Almost all

Egyptian, Middle Kingdom boat model, 1801-1979 B.C. (Dynasty XII), wood coated with painted plaster. Collection of the Virginia Museum of Fine Arts, Richmond. Museum Purchase, The Adolph D. and Wilkins C. Williams Fund.

the dishes in our menus can be prepared ahead of time – even, believe it or not, the French toast. Ingredients for the frittata can be assembled midmorning and finished quickly just before serving. The fruits and marinated vegetables can be chilled the night before, and the coffee can be set up ready to brew.

So, if you suspect there's a touch of Huck Finn in you screaming to get out, come poling down the river with us!

PEACH SMOOTHIE

I cup peeled, chopped fresh peaches
¼ cup plain yogurt
2 teaspoons honey
Dash nutmeg
Milk to thin if needed
Grated lime peel for garnish

Purée peaches in blender. Add yogurt, honey, and nutmeg. Blend well, thinning with milk if too thick to drink.

Chill well and serve with grated lime peel sprinkled on top.

Serves I

CUSTARD FRENCH TOAST WITH ORANGE BUTTER

4 eggs
¼ cup flour
¼ cup sugar
3 cups milk
2 teaspoons vanilla
½ teaspoon cinnamon
8 ¾-inch-thick slices
   firm-texture white bread
Canola or peanut oil for frying

Orange butter:
   ½ stick of butter
   I cup light brown sugar
   I ½ tablespoons grated orange rind

Beat eggs and blend in flour. Add sugar, milk, vanilla, and cinnamon. Beat until completely smooth. Soak bread in batter, turning carefully to soak both sides, until thoroughly saturated.

Heat oil in skillet. Drop bread into pan and fry about 3 minutes on each side until brown and puffed. All this may be made ahead of time and refrigerated. Fifteen minutes before serving, place toast on cookie sheets and heat in 350° oven 15 minutes.

To make orange butter, cream butter, sugar, and rind thoroughly and serve in a bowl to top the toast.

Serves 8

BACON CURLS

To make bacon curls, cook bacon until partially done, but still limp.

When cool enough to handle, roll each strip over your finger and fasten with a toothpick.

Finish cooking in 350° oven until bacon is crisp. Remove toothpick before serving.

Garden-fresh Frittata

4 large eggs
4 cups shredded zucchini squash
2 cups peeled, shredded carrots
½ cup all-purpose flour
¾ cup mayonnaise
1 cup shredded Monterey Jack cheese
½ cup grated Parmesan cheese
¼ cup chopped onion
1 tablespoon chopped fresh basil,
 or 1 teaspoon dried
Freshly ground pepper

Preheat oven to 375°.

Beat eggs. Mix zucchini, carrots, flour, mayonnaise, cheeses, onion, basil, and pepper, and add to eggs.

Pour into buttered quiche pan and bake 30 to 35 minutes or until set.

Serves 6 to 8

Potato Corn Muffins

1 cup yellow cornmeal
4 teaspoons baking powder
1 tablespoon sugar
1 teaspoon salt
1 egg, beaten
1 cup milk
1 cup hot mashed potatoes
2 tablespoons melted shortening

Preheat oven to 400°.

Sift cornmeal, baking powder, sugar, and salt. Combine egg, milk, mashed potatoes, and shortening and pour into dry ingredients, stirring only until moistened.

Grease muffin pans well. Fill ⅔ full. Bake for 25 minutes.

Makes 1 dozen

STICKY ROLL-UPS

1 package dry yeast
¼ cup warm water (110°)
½ cup milk
¼ cup sugar
¼ cup shortening
1 teaspoon salt
3 cups sifted all-purpose flour, divided
1 egg

Filling:
2 tablespoons melted butter
⅓ cup chopped pecans
½ cup sugar
1 ½ teaspoons cinnamon

Soften yeast in warm water. Set aside.

Scald milk and pour over sugar, shortening, and salt. Stir and cool to lukewarm. Add 1 cup flour and mix well. Stir in yeast and egg and beat well. Add 2 cups flour or enough to make a soft dough.

Cover and let rest 10 minutes. On lightly floured surface, knead until satiny, about 8 minutes. Place in greased bowl, turn once, and cover. Let rise in warm place until double.

Roll out to 24 x 7-inch rectangle. Brush dough with butter. Mix pecans, sugar, and cinnamon and sprinkle over dough. Roll up, starting at long side of dough, jelly-roll style. Pinch to seal seam. Cut into 24 slices and place in greased muffin pans, cut side down. May also be rolled into thinner rectangle, cut, and placed in miniature muffin pans.

Cover and let rise about 30 minutes. Preheat oven to 350°. Bake 12 to 15 minutes.

Makes 24

ICED COFFEE, LYNCHBURG STYLE

Strong coffee
Heavy cream, whipped until stiff
Zest of 1 orange, peeled into curls

Brew your favorite coffee and refrigerate.

When ready to serve, pour over ice and garnish with a dollop of whipped cream and a curl of orange zest.

DAFFODIL FESTIVAL
GLOUCESTER

MENUS

Springtime Wine Punch

Mango Slices *with* Toasted Coconut

Swiss Cheese Soufflé *with* Shrimp Sauce

Gazpacho Salad *with* Cucumber Sauce

Basil Baby Limas *and* Peas

Apple Crunch Muffins

Chocolate Delights

Grapefruit Sections *with* Pomegranate Seeds

Tomato Welsh Rarebit *on* English Muffins

Frizzled Ham

Fresh Asparagus *with* Cracked Pepper

Lemon Curd "Sandwiches"

"*O*h, what is so rare as a day in June?" An April day in Gloucester, Virginia, that's what, when the sky is a bluebird's wing and the daffodils are raining gold all over the landscape.

Gloucester has been called the Daffodil Capital of the world, and the golden glow of these harbingers of spring covers huge fields as far as you can see. A picturesque little village, it is rich in history (dating from the early 1600s) and natural beauty. Flowers run riot, as they are wont to do near the sea, so the area is a botanical Eden all summer long.

Gloucester County lies between the York River and Mobjack Bay on the James-York Peninsula. It was designated an official port in 1680, and tobacco and various other goods were shipped from there to England and on to Europe. Gloucester has been bustling ever since, never more so than in April, when the annual Daffodil Festival brings as many as 15,000 visitors. A large arts and crafts show, entertainment, a village decorating show, and wonderful food are all part of this extravaganza.

Floral subjects seem to inspire a special intensity on the part of artists who focus on the natural world. The Museum's recently acquired watercolor, *Anemones and Daffodils* by Henry Roderick Newman (next page), captures a scattering of wildflowers and blossoming trees set against a lush hillside. Fierce precision marks Newman as a leading American-born practitioner of John Ruskin's naturalism. Ruskin, the most influential aesthetic authority of his day, advocated the close scrutiny and exact rendering of natural forms.

Newman had earlier pursued a career in medicine but abandoned it for art. Through careful preparatory studies and a meticulous stipple technique, he incorporated a wealth of clearly rendered botanical information, making each flower an individual portrait. The minute detail and high finish of this watercolor reflect his rational and scientific spirit. At the same time the heady, lyrical color is remarkably sensuous.

Before drinking in all the freshness of spring and the splendor of the flowers, or perhaps as a break if you get an early start, you might enjoy brunch. The menus take advantage of the fresh taste of gazpacho salad, chilled and spicy, and bright green vegetables to enhance the cloudlike Swiss cheese soufflé with its rosy shrimp sauce. The Chocolate Delights add a hint of richness to the otherwise light fare. With a polite nod toward breakfast in the form of tomato Welsh rarebit on English muffins, frizzled ham, and the first green asparagus vibrating with flavor, this second menu is a meal that men, too, will love. We've crowned our menu with jonquil-yellow lemon curd "sandwiches" to celebrate the day.

Think yellow when you plan your table. The flowers are — what else — daffodils! If you have a collection of glass or porcelain animals, you might use them in the center of the table with a ring of short-stemmed jonquils and lemon leaves around them. If you don't have access to the flowers, a bowl or pyramid of lemons and greenery will give you the desired effect. Yellow-and-white china and striped or plaid napkins will guarantee a sunny table, redolent of the glories of spring.

Henry Roderick Newman (American, ca. 1833-1917), *Anemones and Daffodils*, 1884, watercolor on paper. Collection of the Virginia Museum of Fine Arts, Richmond. Museum Purchase, The J. Harwood and Louise B. Cochrane Fund for American Art.

SPRINGTIME WINE PUNCH

I 750-milliliter bottle Sauterne wine
I 6-ounce can frozen pineapple juice
⅓ cup Cointreau liqueur
I 28-ounce bottle ginger ale
Lemon slices for garnish

In large pitcher, mix wine, pineapple juice, and Cointreau. Refrigerate overnight.

Chill ginger ale. At serving time, stir ginger ale into wine mixture. Garnish with lemon slices.

Serves 12

SWISS CHEESE SOUFFLÉ

½ cup butter
6 tablespoons flour
2 cups milk
2 cups grated Swiss cheese
8 eggs, separated
I ½ teaspoons dry mustard
¼ teaspoon cayenne pepper
I teaspoon salt

Preheat oven to 350°.

Melt butter in medium saucepan. Add flour and stir until bubbly. Add milk and slowly bring to boil, stirring constantly until thick. Remove from heat and add cheese. Cool slightly.

Add beaten egg yolks, mustard, pepper, and salt. Cool. Beat egg whites until stiff and fold into cheese mixture.

Pour into buttered 3-quart soufflé or casserole dish. Bake 30 minutes, or place in pan of hot water and bake 1 hour. If the water method is used, the soufflé will hold longer.

Serves 8

SHRIMP SAUCE
The perfect topping for a light soufflé

4 tablespoons butter
4 tablespoons flour
I large fish-flavor bouillon cube
I cup boiling water
I cup milk
¼ teaspoon paprika
I ½ cups shrimp, cooked, peeled, and cut in half

Melt butter in saucepan. Add flour and stir constantly until it bubbles and turns a light golden color. Dissolve bouillon cube in boiling water. Slowly add to roux along with milk. Cook and stir until smooth and thickened. Add paprika and shrimp. Keep warm.

Serve over Swiss cheese soufflé.

GAZPACHO SALAD

1 28-ounce can crushed or stewed tomatoes
2 tablespoons vinegar
2 teaspoons sugar
1 tablespoon butter
Dash salt
4 ½ ounces lemon gelatin
½ cup diced onion
1 cup chopped celery
½ cup chopped green pepper

Cucumber Sauce:
  ¾ cup sour cream
  ¼ cup mayonnaise
  ¼ cup minced onion
  1 cup chopped, seeded cucumber
  Fresh chives for garnish

Cook tomatoes, vinegar, sugar, butter, and salt for 5 minutes. Add gelatin, mixing well and cool. Fold in onion, celery, and green pepper. Pour into a large mold and refrigerate until firm.

To make sauce, mix together sour cream, mayonnaise, onion, and cucumber. Place in a serving dish.

Garnish cucumber sauce with snipped chives and serve as topping.

Serves 12

BASIL BABY LIMAS AND PEAS

2 10-ounce packages frozen baby lima
  beans, thawed
2 10-ounce packages frozen peas, thawed
2 medium onions, sliced and separated
  into thin rings
2 large green peppers, cored and sliced
  into thin rings
2 to 4 teaspoons dried basil
2 teaspoons salt
4 tablespoons butter or margarine
Lettuce leaves to cover casserole

Mix beans, peas, onions, peppers, basil, and salt in a large bowl. Place vegetable mixture in a shallow, buttered 3-quart casserole. Top with butter and completely cover vegetables with lettuce leaves. Cover with lid or foil.

Bake about 45 minutes in 350° oven (do not preheat oven) or until vegetables are tender. Discard lettuce before serving.

Serves 12

APPLE CRUNCH MUFFINS

2 cups sifted flour
3 teaspoons baking powder
½ cup sugar
½ teaspoon salt
3 tablespoons shortening
1 egg, beaten
¾ cup milk
1 cup peeled, chopped tart apple

Topping:
  ⅓ cup brown sugar
  ½ teaspoon cinnamon
  ⅓ cup chopped walnuts

Preheat oven to 400°.

Sift together flour, baking powder, sugar, and salt. Cut in shortening.

Combine egg and milk, and add to flour mixture. Mix until flour is just moist. Fold in apple.

Grease muffin pan and fill half full. Combine topping ingredients and sprinkle over batter. Bake 25 minutes.

Makes 1 dozen

CHOCOLATE DELIGHTS

1 pound sweet milk chocolate
2 1-ounce squares unsweetened chocolate
½ teaspoon powdered instant coffee
1 cup chopped pecans
1 cup chopped dates
½ cup golden raisins
¼ teaspoon salt
5 cups cornflakes

❧ Melt both chocolates over hot water in double boiler. Add coffee.

❧ Combine pecans, dates, raisins, salt, and cornflakes. Add to melted chocolates and stir quickly and carefully until well blended and all cornflakes are covered.

❧ Drop from teaspoon onto wax paper. Chill until firm. Keeps a long time in the refrigerator.

❧ Makes about 3½ dozen

TOMATO WELSH RAREBIT

2 tablespoons butter or margarine
3 tablespoons all-purpose flour
⅔ cup beer
1 14 ½-ounce can whole tomatoes, drained and chopped
10 ounces extra sharp cheese, grated
½ teaspoon dry mustard
1 ½ teaspoons Worcestershire sauce
½ teaspoon Tabasco
2 slices toast per serving or toasted English muffins
Italian parsley or other parsley for garnish

❧ Combine butter and flour in heavy saucepan and cook over low heat, whisking about 3 minutes. Add beer and tomatoes. Boil and whisk 3 minutes.

❧ Turn heat to low and add cheese, dry mustard, Worcestershire sauce, and Tabasco. Cook until hot, but do not boil. Serve over toast or muffins.

❧ Can also be spooned over cooked lobster, shrimp, crabmeat, or tuna; sliced hard-boiled or poached eggs; broccoli, cauliflower, or asparagus; ham, chicken, or turkey.

❧ Serves 4 to 6

Lemon Curd "Sandwiches"

1 cup butter, room temperature
2 cups sugar
4 eggs, well beaten
3 cups flour
2 teaspoons baking powder
1 scant cup milk
1 teaspoon vanilla
Lemon curd
Powdered sugar

Preheat oven to 350°.

Cream butter and sugar, then add eggs. Sift together flour and baking powder. Add flour mixture and milk alternately. Add vanilla. Mix well.

Bake in a greased and floured 13 x 17½-inch jelly-roll pan for 12 to 15 minutes. Remove from oven when cake springs back when touched. Cool slightly. Turn onto cake rack to cool.

Using a 1½-inch biscuit cutter, cut whole cake into circles. Slice each round in half and put 1 teaspoon lemon curd on bottom half. Cover with top half. When all rounds have been completed, sprinkle with powdered sugar.

If not served right away, refrigerate. Freezes well.

Makes 4 dozen

Lemon Curd

5 egg yolks
1 egg white
¼ cup lemon juice
1 cup sugar
3 tablespoons butter

Mix all ingredients together well, then simmer in double boiler until thick and clear, stirring constantly. Refrigerate in jar for use as needed.

Can also be used over hot toast, hot biscuits, or in small tarts.

Lunches

Easter Luncheon

Menu

Mimosas

Greek Shrimp *and* Rice

Broiled Tomatoes

Whole Green Beans
with Herbed Butter

Russian Easter Buns

Sherbet Eggs *in a* Basket

Peter Carl Fabergé (Russian, 1846-1920), *Czarevitch Egg*, 1912, workmaster: Henrik Wigstrom (1862-ca. 1930), lapis lazuli, gold, platinum, and diamonds. Collection of the Virginia Museum of Fine Arts, Richmond. Bequest of Lillian Thomas Pratt.

*E*aster, happy Easter, the most glorious day of the Christian calendar! This celebration marks rebirth and renewal, both of the earth and of the spirit, and sings out joy to the world as much as Christmas. As the oldest Christian observance (after Sunday, which, as the weekly celebration of the resurrection, is regarded as a "little Easter"), Easter coincides with the more ancient Jewish Passover. The word Easter is of unknown origin, but it seems to have been derived from Eostre, the Anglo-Saxon goddess of spring.

Eggs, originally forbidden to be eaten during Lent, have come to be one of the most prominent symbols of new life and resurrection associated with Easter. Traditional egg-painting in Europe focused on the butterfly, the phoenix rising from the ashes, flowers, and newborn animals, all symbolic of new life. Peter Carl Fabergé (1846–1920) took the egg to its artistic pinnacle in his commissions from the czars of Russia. Shown here is an example from the Virginia Museum's fabulous Fabergé collection. The *Czarevitch Egg* from the Fabergé workshop is the work of Henrik Wigstrom, a talented Swedish Finn who assumed responsibility for the creation of the imperial Easter eggs in 1903. The elaborate and exquisite gold cage-work of shells, scrolls, flower baskets, and cupids overlays the lapis lazuli shell. The top opens to reveal a removable double-headed Russian eagle of platinum and rose diamonds,

encasing a portrait miniature of the seven-year-old Czarevitch Alexis. Altogether this is not your ordinary Easter egg!

Clothes are often another celebratory symbol of Easter. As Gertrude Mueller Nelson observed in her book *To Dance With God: Family Ritual and Community Celebration*, everyone "needs something new and springlike to wear as a reminder of our baptismal garments and our new beginnings." *The Plumed Hat* (page 39), a painting by Kees van Dongen in the Virginia Museum collection, would surely be the grandest in any Easter parade. The Dutch van Dongen, who later painted portraits of famous people from Anatole France to Brigitte Bardot, has been associated with the Fauves, who used bright colors in bold, flat shapes. The dynamic figure in this stylish canvas has a hint of caricature both in her pose and in her enormous hat. Her tiny dog and the haute couture offer whimsical comments on Parisian society.

Of course, what would Easter be without a bunny? The hare, symbol of fertility in ancient Egypt and later in Europe, in this country becomes the Easter rabbit, that engaging, elusive creature who hides eggs for children and leaves goody baskets on doorsteps. The grandest rabbit of them all surely lives in the Virginia Museum. Barry Flanagan's *Large Leaping Hare* (next page) is a gargantuan gilded bronze creature that is both illogical and captivating. The hare's Welsh creator is fascinated "with the device of investing an animal — a hare especially — with the expressive attributes of a human being. The ears, for instance, are really able to convey more than the squint in the eye of a figure or the grimace on the face of a model." Leaping through the air, this intriguing figure soars above the earth, yet is tied to it by beams of iron. Like man, it is a creature of both earth and heaven.

Every region has its own special Easter traditions. In Richmond, *Easter on Parade* on Monument Avenue is a family celebration with activities for all ages, a wide variety of music and food, roving performers, and an Easter-bonnet contest. It is one of Richmond's favorite street festivals, attended by thousands of residents from all parts of the city.

For Easter celebrations anywhere, the climax of the day is the holiday meal. The table should be a feast for the eyes. Ours is set for luncheon and arrayed in pristine linen and lace with heirloom china, glittering crystal, and the luminous purity of Easter lilies. For this occasion, we offer the best and the freshest of spring foods: golden mimosas for a toast, Greek shrimp and rice, crisp yet tender whole green beans, individual edible Easter baskets, and luscious Russian Easter buns, iced with the Greek initials XB for the traditional Easter saying, "Christ Is Risen." Alleluia!

Barry Flanagan (Welsh, born 1941) *Large Leaping Hare*, 1982, gilt bronze (from an edition of four). Collection of the Virginia Museum of Fine Arts, Richmond. Gift of Sydney and Frances Lewis.

MIMOSAS

3 ounces fresh orange juice
3 ounces champagne
½ ounce triple sec liqueur
Fresh strawberries for garnish
Mint sprigs for garnish

Mix together juice, champagne, and triple sec. Pour into chilled wine glasses half filled with ice.

Garnish each glass with a strawberry and a sprig of mint.

Serves 1

GREEK SHRIMP AND RICE

6 tablespoons olive oil
⅔ cup chopped onion
2 28-ounce cans Italian tomatoes, drained and chopped
1 cup dry white wine
2 teaspoons dried oregano
2 cups sliced mushrooms
2 pounds shrimp, peeled and deveined
Salt and pepper to taste

Greek-style Rice:
4 tablespoons olive oil
½ cup chopped onion
1 cup pignolias (pine nuts)
2 cups long-grain rice
2 14 ½-ounce cans chicken broth
1 cup crumbled feta cheese
6 tablespoons minced fresh mint or
   2 tablespoons dried mint
Salt and pepper to taste

Heat oil in large, heavy skillet over medium heat and add onion and sauté until translucent, about 8 minutes. Add tomatoes, wine, oregano, and simmer until thickened, about 5 minutes.

Add mushrooms and shrimp and cook about 4 minutes. Season with salt and pepper.

To make rice, heat oil in medium-sized, heavy saucepan over medium heat. Add onion and pignolias and sauté until onion is transparent, about 5 minutes. Add rice and broth and bring to a boil. Reduce heat to low, cover and cook until broth is absorbed, about 20 minutes.

Fluff with fork and add cheese and mint. Season with salt and pepper.

Serves 8

Kees van Dongen (Dutch, 1877-1968), *The Plumed Hat,* 1910, oil on canvas.Collection of the Virginia Museum of Fine Arts, Richmond. Collection of Mr. and Mrs. Paul Mellon.

BROILED TOMATOES

¼ cup sour cream
¼ cup mayonnaise
2 tablespoons Parmesan cheese
1 ½ tablespoons lemon juice
½ tablespoon chopped parsley
2 tablespoons grated onion
5 tomatoes

Mix sour cream, mayonnaise, cheese, lemon juice, parsley, and onion.

Top tomatoes which have been cut in half with sour cream mixture. Broil until bubbly.

Serves 10

HERBED BUTTER
Dresses up even the plainest vegetables

½ cup softened butter or margarine
2 small to medium cloves garlic, crushed
¼ cup grated Parmesan cheese
¼ teaspoon dried basil
¼ teaspoon dried oregano

Combine all ingredients, mix thoroughly, and put in ramekin.

Delicious served on slices of French bread. Substituting 1 teaspoon each fresh herb in place of dried makes it even better.

RUSSIAN EASTER BUNS

½ cup sugar, divided
1 package dry yeast
¼ cup hot water
½ teaspoon salt
2 eggs, beaten
⅓ cup soft margarine or shortening
¾ cup warm milk
1 teaspoon almond extract
3 drops yellow food coloring (optional)
3 ½ to 4 cups flour
⅓ cup raisins
⅔ cup finely chopped citron or mixed peels
¼ cup finely chopped almonds
Melted margarine

Glaze:
2 cups powdered sugar
¼ cup hot milk
Pinch salt
1 tablespoon soft butter
¼ teaspoon almond extract

Mix together ¼ cup sugar, yeast, and water in a large bowl. Stir until mixture dissolves. Add salt, eggs, ¼ cup sugar, margarine, milk, 1 teaspoon almond extract, and food coloring to yeast mixture.

Beat in flour until dough is thick enough to handle. Combine raisins, citron, and almonds, and stir into dough.

Knead on lightly floured board until smooth and elastic. Place in greased bowl and cover. Allow to rise in warm place until doubled in bulk, about I to I½ hours. Punch down and turn onto floured board. Roll out to ½-inch thickness. Cut into rounds with 2½-inch biscuit cutter, form into balls, and place in rows on greased baking sheet. Brush with melted margarine. Allow to rise in warm place until doubled in bulk.

Preheat oven to 375°. Bake about 15 minutes or until lightly browned.

To make glaze, sift powdered sugar into small bowl. Add hot milk, salt, butter, and ¼ teaspoon almond extract. Beat until smooth. Spoon over hot buns, saving ½ cup glaze.

When glaze is set and buns have cooled a bit, put remaining glaze into small cake decorating bag. Write the Russian letters XB (Christ has risen) on each bun.

Makes 15

SHERBET "EGGS" IN A BASKET
An edible Easter basket

¼ cup margarine
40 large marshmallows, or 4 cups miniature
5 cups Rice Krispies cereal
I quart orange sherbet
I quart lime sherbet
I quart raspberry sherbet
I quart pineapple sherbet

In a large saucepan, melt margarine and marshmallows over low heat, stirring constantly. Remove from heat and add cereal, stirring until well coated.

Thoroughly butter medium-sized mixing bowl. Firmly and evenly press the cereal mixture over entire inner surface of bowl. Chill several hours. To remove basket, dip bowl into hot water for a few seconds. Carefully loosen edges, and transfer basket from bowl to a plate. Gently press sides of basket until they are firm again.

Soften sherbet just enough to shape into "eggs" with 2 tablespoons. Place "eggs" on chilled cookie sheet and freeze.

Immediately before serving, arrange "eggs" in basket so that the various colors are visible above rim. Serve "eggs" with a piece of the basket.

Serves 8 to 10

CARD PARTY LUNCHEON

Whenever you sit down at your card table, you're "dealing with" one of the oldest games in the world. For at least 600 years in Europe, and many centuries more in the Orient, playing cards have been used for gaming, conjuring, and divination. During the 20th century, however, they have served mainly for casual pastimes.

There are references to playing cards in China as early as A.D. 969; but long before that (early in the T'ang Dynasty), the Chinese had paper money that was so similar in design to playing cards that the two may have emerged almost simultaneously there. Originally the cards and the money may even have been identical. The logical implication is that they were probably part of the graphic arts wherever those arts emerged – Egypt, Arabia, China, Hindustan – all of which are places where, at one time or another, playing cards were said to have originated.

Playing cards were probably first used more for divination than for gaming, as they were associated with religious rites and symbols. Hindu cards had ten suits representing the ten incarnations of Vishnu. Throughout the Middle Ages, the cards were used in Europe and Asia for fortunetelling, a practice that continues today. A Saracen card game called Naib was brought to Italy in the 14th century. It is no coincidence that naibi is

Hebrew for "sorcery." Such cards may have been brought home by returning crusaders, introduced in Spain and Italy by Saracen invaders, or carried to Eastern Europe by gypsies and Tartars – makes the weekly bridge game a bit more alluring and mysterious, doesn't it?

The earliest cards made in Europe were tarots. These were picture cards, unlike cards from the East, which were divided into suits and numbered, as are modern cards. They were used for fortunetelling, as they are today. Sometime in the 14th century, the 22 picture tarots were combined with the 56 oriental number cards, becoming the precursors of the decks we have today. They were beautifully designed, elaborately hand-painted, and obviously too costly for all but the aristocracy. Early in the 15th century, wood engravers began printing cards, and their use spread rapidly among the rank and file. These cards were colored by stencils and dyes, a process that remained in use for more than 350 years. Today they are printed by offset or lithography.

Playing cards is a national pastime in the United States, and when times are bad and money is scarce, the volume of deck purchases goes up. Card playing is an inexpensive diversion – unless high stakes are involved! Perhaps because of this, it has been viewed both

Margaret Macdonald (Scottish, 1865-1933), *The Four Queens*, 1909, paint, gesso, wood.
Collection of the Virginia Museum of Fine Arts, Richmond. Gift of Sydney and Frances Lewis.

benignly and severely: a 14th-century monk's manuscript deemed it a "harmless pastime," while the Puritans considered playing cards to be the "Devil's Picture Book"!

When you take into account the number of period card tables available internationally through antique dealers and auction houses, you realize that from loo to whist, rook to poker, and gin rummy to bridge, we have been and are a card-playing world.

At times, playing cards have provided both a diversion and an aura of status. By the turn of the last century, many large, affluent homes boasted a "card room." In the collection of the Virginia Museum, originally intended to decorate such a room, are mystical and mildly menacing depictions of the "ladies of the deck," *The Four Queens* by Margaret Macdonald.

Macdonald was an accomplished artist and designer who often collaborated with her husband, Charles Rennie Mackintosh, a leader of the Arts and Crafts Movement in Scotland. Among their most notable projects was the Glasgow Tea Room.

The Four Queens were commissioned by Catherine Cranston for the card room at "Hous'hill," her rambling old house on the outskirts of Glasgow. The panels, which were probably set into the walls, are made of wood and gesso, elaborately colored and gilded.

Whether your card game is strictly for fun or deadly serious, it can require strenuous mental concentration. A break in the intensity – usually in the form of a light luncheon or late supper – is welcome. We give you two card party menus, both light and easy to pre-

pare; no one needs soporific food during a rubber of bridge!

Tomato phyllo, a variation of the French "pizza," pisalladiere, is balanced by the sharpness and crunch of the marinated broccoli, with its raisins and very crisp bacon adding sweet and smoky touches. In the dessert, macaroons and peaches combine for a synergistic marriage of two fabulous flavors.

For another time, the cold chicken and wild rice salad, with its added texture of celery, raisins, red pepper, and the bite of balsamic vinegar, is a refreshing counterpoint to asparagus and cheese biscuits. The citrus velvet dessert is cool, silky, and not too sweet.

With a card party, you and your guests can indulge in two of America's favorite pastimes, gaming and eating. So let the play begin!

CHICKEN AND WILD RICE SALAD

⅔ cup uncooked wild rice
¼ teaspoon salt
2 cups boiling water
3 large boneless halves of chicken breast,
   cooked and cubed
1 large tart apple, cored, unpeeled,
   and chopped
⅓ small red onion, minced
½ large red sweet pepper, cored and diced
½ cup dried currants
½ cup diced celery
½ cup pecan pieces, toasted
2 tablespoons balsamic vinegar
2 tablespoons olive oil
Salt and pepper to taste

❈ Add rice and salt to boiling water and cook until tender, about 35 minutes. Drain any remaining water.

❈ Transfer rice to large bowl and add chicken, apple, onion, red pepper, currants, celery, pecans, vinegar, and olive oil. Season with salt and pepper to taste.

❈ May be served cold or warm by heating in microwave on High for 3 minutes.

❈ Serves 4 to 6

CHEESE BISCUITS
Keep an extra batch in the freezer.

2 cups sifted all-purpose flour
4 teaspoons baking powder
2 teaspoons sugar
½ teaspoon salt
½ teaspoon cream of tartar
½ cup vegetable shortening
⅓ pound extra-sharp cheese, grated
⅔ cup milk

❈ Sift dry ingredients into bowl. Cut in shortening, then cheese. Add milk. Mix to form dough and roll to ¾-inch thickness. Cut into 2-inch rounds.

❈ Freeze rounds on a cookie sheet, then put into plastic freezer bag until ready to bake.

❈ Preheat oven to 300°.

❈ Bake frozen 10 minutes, then at 450° 10 minutes. If not frozen, bake at 425° about 10 to 12 minutes.

❈ Makes 1 dozen

CITRUS VELVET

1 envelope plain gelatin
1 cup water, divided
2 eggs, separated
¾ cup sugar, divided
¼ teaspoon salt
1 6-ounce can frozen orange juice
    concentrate
2 teaspoons lemon juice
⅓ cup heavy cream
Mint, orange zest, or toasted almonds for
    garnish

Soften gelatin in ¼ cup warm water. Combine egg yolks, ¾ cup water, ½ cup sugar, and salt. Cook over hot water in a small double boiler until it coats the spoon, stirring constantly. Add gelatin mixture and stir until dissolved. Remove from heat and stir in orange juice concentrate and lemon juice. Chill until slightly thick.

Beat egg whites and ¼ cup sugar until stiff. Whip cream and fold into chilled mixture, then fold in egg whites.

Pour into crystal bowl to congeal. At serving time, garnish with fresh mint, orange zest, or toasted almonds.

Instead of frozen orange juice, you can use frozen lime, lemonade, or any citrus flavor.

Serves 8

TOMATO PHYLLO LUNCHEON DISH
A blend of Mediterranean flavors

½ stick butter or margarine, melted
7 whole sheets phyllo dough
1 cup grated Parmesan cheese, divided
1 cup grated mozzarella cheese
1 cup thinly sliced onion
5 or 6 garden-ripe tomatoes, thinly sliced
Dried thyme
Dried oregano

Preheat oven to 375°.

Brush baking sheet with butter or margarine and place 1 sheet of phyllo on baking sheet. Brush phyllo with melted butter and sprinkle all over with 1 tablespoon of Parmesan cheese. Repeat with next 5 sheets of phyllo dough. On seventh sheet of dough, brush with butter, sprinkle with mozzarella cheese, then arrange onion slices on top. Layer tomato slices over onions.

Sprinkle with thyme and oregano and remaining Parmesan cheese.

Bake in center of oven 30 to 35 minutes or until edges are golden brown. Cut in serving pieces with sharp knife or pizza wheel.

Makes 4 to 5 main-course or 8 to 10 first-course servings

MARINATED BROCCOLI

1½ pounds fresh broccoli
½ cup finely chopped onion
½ cup golden raisins
¾ cup mayonnaise
¼ cup sugar
2 tablespoons vinegar or lemon juice
6 strips well-cooked bacon, drained and
    crumbled

Cut broccoli florets into bite-size pieces. Remove tough outer part of remaining stalks and slice stalks crosswise into very thin pieces. Add onions and raisins.

Mix mayonnaise, sugar, and vinegar, and pour over broccoli mixture.

Refrigerate 24 hours, stirring occasionally.

Sprinkle with bacon just before serving.

Serves 12

POPPY SEED MUFFINS

½ cup margarine
1 cup sugar
2 eggs
1 cup sour cream
1 teaspoon vanilla
2 cups flour
3 teaspoons poppy seeds
½ teaspoon salt
¼ teaspoon baking soda

Preheat oven to 400°.

Cream margarine and sugar. Add eggs and beat. Stir in sour cream and vanilla and mix well.

Combine flour, poppy seeds, salt, and baking soda, and stir into the sour cream mixture. Spoon batter into greased muffin tins and bake 15 to 20 minutes.

Makes 1 dozen

PEACH MACAROON DELIGHT
*A delicious dessert that can be
prepared ahead of time*

18 medium-sized macaroons
1 quart peach ice cream
½ cup frozen grated coconut
½ 2¼-ounce package slivered almonds
½ cup light rum
Fresh sliced peaches (optional)

Line 9-inch ring mold with macaroons.

Slightly soften ice cream and add coconut, almonds, and rum. Mash into ring mold. Freeze until solid.

When ready to serve, turn upside down on platter or plate, and leave several minutes, or until unmolded. Slice and serve with fresh sliced peaches.

Serves 8

Working Persons' Lunches

*I*f you are a member of America's work force, and that includes most of us, going to a restaurant for lunch every day can be: a) boring; b) fattening; c) expensive.

All of the above are reasons for a growing new trend: bringing your lunch to work. Many offices have installed microwave ovens, so that foods can be cooked or reheated "in-house." Many new office buildings have parklike surroundings with built-in seats or benches where people can enjoy a lunch break and socialize — or put together a deal! In fine weather, the grassy knoll at Richmond's James Center is crowded with people doing just that. Such a welcome mix of landscape with commercial buildings for the workers' benefit and the city's beautification is fast becoming the norm. Here utility and aesthetics are both compatible and people-oriented.

When it comes to working people, one of the most evocative subjects in the Virginia Museum collection is Duane Hanson's *Hard-Hat Construction Worker* (next page). This life-size figure of a working man with his lunch pail, made of painted polyester resin, clothes, wood, metal, and plastic, is so incredibly realistic that many viewers stop short, startled, thinking they have interrupted him at his lunch in the gallery. Hanson comments: "The subject matter I like best deals with the familiar American types of today. . . . As a realist, I'm not interested in the human form . . . but rather a face or body which has suffered like some weather-worn landscape the erosion of time."

Claes Oldenburg's *Typewriter Eraser* (page 52) is another object that captures our interest as it revises our perceptions of the familiar. The sculpture is of a giant eraser, the kind once found in offices everywhere next to the secretary's typewriter. It was originally commissioned for a site on West 57th Street in the heart of New York's business district. Oldenburg was fascinated by the many shapes of erasers and their relationship to the human form. This eraser sits on one edge at a slight angle, its bristles bent and frayed from use. The piece suggests many interpretations. Perhaps today, with typewriters now replaced by self-correcting word processors, we can see this sculpture as a tribute to all the secretaries and typists who once corrected countless mistakes on endless reams and who now can do it all without ever touching the paper!

Putting together the working lunch can be a challenge. But while it may tax your ingenuity, it can also spur your creativity, and it's a great way to use leftovers. Our suggestions use both fresh and "recycled" ingredients, borscht and beef salad (last night's vegetables and roast?), glazed corned beef (from the deli or your own kitchen), chicken-rice salad (poach a couple of extra breasts) and ham biscuits, which can be made ahead in quantity and frozen. Pull them right from the freezer in the morning, so they'll be thawed and ready to eat by lunchtime.

There are many different "envelopes" besides bread for stuffing your luncheon ingredients: cold crêpes wrapped around paper-thin slices of ham and chicken with curried mayonnaise (or try pork tenderloin and watercress); large iceberg lettuce leaves filled with taco ingredients and rolled into bundles; or even BLTs in pita pockets. Or use two slices of processed Swiss, Monterey Jack, or cheddar cheese and sandwich your favorite vegetables or meats between. Soups can be made and frozen in individual portions, then just zapped in the microwave while you drink your morning coffee, and poured in a thermos.

With a little thought and advance preparation, you can vary your luncheon routine, eat healthier, and use the money you save on a splurge!

Duane Hanson (American, born 1925) *Hard-Hat Construction Worker,* 1970, painted polyester resin, clothes, wood, metal, and plastic. Collection of the Virginia Museum of Fine Arts, Richmond. Gift of Sydney and Frances Lewis.

GRILLED TUNA SALAD
Grill an extra tuna steak for lunch.

1 6-ounce grilled tuna steak, flaked (saved
    from last night's dinner)
2 hard-cooked eggs, coarsely chopped
¼ cup finely chopped celery
1 teaspoon dried onion flakes
1 tablespoon sweet pickle relish
3 tablespoons mayonnaise
¼ teaspoon lemon pepper seasoning
2 tablespoons chopped water chestnuts

Combine all ingredients and mix well. Cover
and chill.

Serve on lettuce or make a sourdough bread
sandwich.

Serves 3 to 4

QUICK SOUP
Homemade soup in only 5 minutes

1 46-ounce can 100% vegetable juice
1 cup sour cream
1 teaspoon dried onion flakes
1 teaspoon Worcestershire sauce
Salt and pepper to taste
Chopped chives

Mix vegetable juice, sour cream, onion
flakes, Worcestershire sauce, salt, and pepper
in blender or food processor until smooth.
Chill.

Sprinkle with chives before serving.

Serves 6

COLD BEEF AND VEGETABLE SALAD WITH DIJON DRESSING
Last night's leftover beef is today's lunch.

Dijon Dressing:
    ¼ cup vegetable oil
    5 teaspoons vinegar
    1 teaspoon Dijon mustard
    Dash Tabasco
    Salt and pepper to taste

1 cup bite-size pieces rare roast beef
¼ cup cooked green beans
2 thin slices purple onion
1 cup bite-size pieces cooked red potatoes
6 small green olives
3 cherry tomatoes, halved

To make the dressing, combine oil, vinegar,
mustard, Tabasco, salt, and pepper. Mix well.
Let stand at room temperature for at least 2
hours.

In a large bowl, mix beef, green beans,
onion, potatoes, olives, and tomatoes.

Add dressing to salad and toss. Serve on lettuce.

Serves 4 to 6

PASTA AND BEAN SALAD
A do-ahead salad

I cup cooked kidney beans
I sweet red pepper, cored and chopped
I green pepper, cored and chopped
8 ounces bow-tie pasta, cooked and drained
¼ pound bean sprouts, rinsed and drained
¼ cup sliced scallions

Dressing:
3 tablespoons lemon juice
½ cup olive oil
I tablespoon soy sauce
¼ teaspoon pepper
¼ teaspoon salt
¼ teaspoon sugar

Place all salad ingredients in salad bowl.
Mix dressing ingredients and toss with salad.

Better if prepared several hours in advance.

Serves 6 to 8

HEALTH NUT COOKIE
A nutritionally satisfying sweet

½ cup softened margarine
½ cup packed brown sugar
¾ teaspoon vanilla
I egg
¼ cup all-purpose flour
½ cup whole-wheat flour
½ teaspoon baking soda
¼ teaspoon salt
I cup quick oatmeal
¾ cup cornflakes
⅓ cup currants
3 tablespoons toasted sunflower seeds
½ cup chopped nuts

Preheat oven to 375°.

Cream margarine and sugar until light and fluffy. Add vanilla and egg. Mix well.

Combine flours, baking soda, and salt, and add to creamed mixture. Add oatmeal, cornflakes, currants, sunflower seeds, and nuts. Mix well.

Drop dough by tablespoon onto greased cookie sheet 2 inches apart.

Bake 6 to 8 minutes.

Makes 2 dozen

Claes Oldenburg (American; born Sweden, 1929), *Typewriter Eraser*, 1976, aluminum, stainless steel, and ferrocement; one of an edition of three. Collection of the Virginia Museum of Fine Arts, Richmond. Gift of Sydney and Frances Lewis.

Picnics

MENU

Blueberry Soup

Celebration Turkey Salad

Apple Date Muffins

Sliced Tomatoes

Carrot Salad

Fruited Cheese Spread *on*
Briggs Whole-Wheat Bread

Butter Cake

FOURTH OF JULY PICNIC
DANVILLE

*T*he picnic as an entertainment form is part of the fabric of American life. Any excuse will do: the first soft day of spring, a birthday, a day too hot to cook, a football game, or the last day of summer, when it is still warm and golden, but the leaves are flushed with color.

The quintessential American picnic day, however, is the Fourth of July. All the props for a party are there: parades, speeches, music, fireworks, and most of all, the gift of our freedom to celebrate.

The menu, of course, is red, white, and blue. It is also a gift of freedom—for the cook. Everything may be prepared ahead and chilled: cold blueberry soup, celebration turkey salad, ruby-red sliced tomatoes from the garden, fruited cheese spread, with butter cake and succulent whole strawberries for dessert.

If you are such a purist that anything but fried chicken, cole slaw, corn on the cob, and apple pie spell sacrilege, that's all right. You can add the blueberry soup as an exciting twist to a traditional menu. Or make a patriot's pie, an oblong of puff pastry filled with rows of blueberries and raspberries and piped with Kentucky bourbon–spiked whipped cream.

The setting for our picnic is Danville, Virginia, where in addition to all the traditional festivities, there is the added fun and excitement of an annual hot-air balloon race. A Victorian flower of a city, Danville sits in the middle of the state, near the North Carolina border. Its wealth, vitality, and stability are derived from both the tobacco and the textile industries, and its "Millionaire's Row" of Main Street mansions is a wondrous display of Victorian architecture. For history buffs, the Sutherlin House, now restored to its original splendor, was the last capitol of the Confederacy, and little Nancy Langhorne, who went on to become Lady Astor and the first woman to sit in the British House of Commons, was born just down the street.

And what better painting to capture the American spirit than Walt Kuhn's *Salute* (next page) from the Virginia Museum collections, with its "spit and polish," its bright brassy colors, its assured determination. Kuhn was born in Brooklyn, the son of a Bavarian father and a Spanish mother. It was her fascination with the theater, in the words of Philip R. Adams, Kuhn's biographer, that "addicted her son to show business of all kinds," especially vaudeville, variety shows, and the circus. How fitting that Kuhn should convey the essence of the youthful confidence, the chin-up attitude of the American character. Adams comments:

Many people are perplexed by the fact that almost all of the artist's human subjects are never the stars but clowns, acrobats, show-girls, the overworked and underpaid proletariat of show business, whether on the stage or in the circus. They have given up hope of ever seeing their name in lights, but they keep on with the arduous discipline their trade imposes on them and they would not have it otherwise. Pride of profession knows no class distinctions and is self-sustaining.

The show must go on! So here's to picnics, from backyards to tailgates, country meadows to beaches, penthouse terraces to riverside settings. They're a four-star, show-stopping way to celebrate life.

Walt Kuhn (American, 1877-1949), *Salute*, 1934, oil on canvas. Collection of the Virginia Museum of Fine Arts, Richmond. Museum Purchase, The Adolph D. and Wilkins C. Williams Fund.

BLUEBERRY SOUP

2 cups fresh blueberries
2 cups water
I cup sugar
I ½-inch thick slice lemon
I cinnamon stick
I 8-ounce carton sour cream

Mix blueberries, water, sugar, lemon slice, and cinnamon stick in saucepan and boil carefully 20 minutes. Remove lemon slice and cinnamon stick and press berry mixture through strainer. Chill purée 4 hours.

Stir in sour cream and refrigerate until serving time.

Serves 6

CELEBRATION TURKEY SALAD

I 6-lb turkey breast
2 10½-ounce cans chicken broth
2 cups water
2 onions studded with 4 whole cloves
I rib celery
4 carrots, peeled and cut in thirds
2 teaspoons salt
10 peppercorns
I bay leaf
¼ cup oil
½ cup lemon juice
I tablespoon onion juice
2 ½ teaspoons dried tarragon or
    2 ½ tablespoons fresh
¾ cup chopped scallions
¼ cup chopped parsley
I teaspoon salt
¼ teaspoon pepper
2 cups mayonnaise
½ cup heavy cream
6 ribs celery, chopped
2 cups drained pineapple chunks or
    sweet fresh pineapple
Lettuce cups
Slivered almonds for garnish

In large pot, cover turkey breast with broth and water. Add onion, cloves, rib of celery, carrots, salt, peppercorns, and bay leaf. Bring to boil, reduce heat, and simmer covered I hour or until done. Cool in broth I to 2 hours. Skin and remove turkey from bones. Cut into bite-size pieces.

Place in large bowl, add oil and toss gently. Mix lemon juice, onion juice, tarragon, scallions, parsley, salt, and pepper. Fold into chopped turkey and chill. When ready to serve, mix mayonnaise with cream. Add to turkey along with celery and pineapple. Mix well.

Serve in lettuce cups garnished with slivered almonds. Chicken breasts may be substituted.

Serves 8 to I0

APPLE DATE MUFFINS
Particularly good with poultry salads

1 ½ cups sifted flour
3 teaspoons baking powder
3 tablespoons sugar
½ teaspoon salt
½ cup chopped dates
2 eggs, beaten
⅔ cup milk
½ cup applesauce
3 tablespoons melted butter

Topping:
⅓ cup flour
⅓ cup sugar
¼ teaspoon cinnamon
¼ cup cold margarine

Preheat oven to 400°.

Sift together flour, baking powder, sugar, and salt. Stir dates into dry ingredients.

Combine eggs, milk, applesauce, and butter. Add to dry ingredients, stirring only until moistened.

Grease muffin pans and fill ⅔ full.

To make topping, combine dry ingredients and cut in cold margarine until crumbly. Sprinkle on top of muffin batter and bake 15 to 20 minutes.

Makes 1 dozen

CARROT SALAD

4 cups thinly sliced carrots
½ cup minced onion
1 ½ tablespoons wine vinegar
1 ½ tablespoons cider vinegar
¾ teaspoon salt
½ teaspoon sugar
¼ teaspoon pepper
1 teaspoon dried dill weed or 1 tablespoon minced fresh

In a medium saucepan, boil carrots in salted water until crisp-tender. Drain.

Mix onion, vinegars, salt, sugar, pepper, and dill weed, and toss with carrots. Refrigerate several hours until flavors meld.

Serves 6 to 8

FRUITED CHEESE SPREAD

½ cup dried apricots
1 cup water
1 pound Monterey Jack cheese, shredded
8 ounces cream cheese, softened
½ cup dry sherry
1 teaspoon poppy seeds
½ teaspoon seasoned salt
½ cup golden raisins, chopped
¼ cup pitted dates, chopped
Milk to thin if needed

Soak apricots in water 2 hours. Drain and chop.

Blend cheeses and add sherry, poppy seeds, and seasoned salt. Mix well. Fold in apricots, raisins, and dates, and mix well.

If too dry to spread, add enough milk to thin mixture.

Briggs Whole-Wheat Bread

6 cups whole-wheat flour
¾ cup sugar
1 ½ teaspoons salt
1 ½ teaspoons baking soda
4 teaspoons baking powder
2 eggs
3 tablespoons shortening
3 cups buttermilk

❄ Preheat oven to 350°.

❄ Mix all ingredients in large mixing bowl. Put into 2 greased 9 x 5 x 3-inch loaf pans and let set 10 minutes. Bake about 35 to 45 minutes.

❄ Loaves freeze well.

❄ Makes 2 loaves

Butter Cake

3 cups flour
1 teaspoon baking powder
1 teaspoon salt
½ teaspoon baking soda
1 cup butter
2 cups sugar
4 eggs
1 cup buttermilk
2 teaspoons vanilla

Butter sauce:
1 cup sugar
¼ cup orange juice
½ cup butter
1 teaspoon orange extract

❄ Preheat oven to 325°.

❄ Sift together flour, baking powder, salt, and soda.

❄ Cream butter and gradually add sugar. Add eggs, one at a time, beating well after each addition.

❄ Combine buttermilk and vanilla. Add alternately with dry ingredients to creamed mixture, beginning and ending with dry ingredients. Blend well after each addition.

❄ Grease well 3 8 x 4 x 3-inch loaf pans. Divide batter evenly among pans and bake 60 to 65 minutes.

❄ To make butter sauce, heat sugar, orange juice, and butter until butter melts. Do not boil. Add orange extract.

❄ When cakes are done, prick with fork and pour butter sauce over cakes.

❄ Cool cakes in pans.

❄ Makes 3 cakes

MONTPELIER HUNT RACES
ORANGE COUNTY

MENU

Pumpkin Bisque

Chicken Drumettes *with* Peanut Sauce

Marinated Pork Loin *with* Plum Sauce

Party Rye Bread

Frances Lambert's Chafing-Dish Crab
with Toast Rounds

Marinated Tomato, Feta, *and* Pepper Salad

Breadbasket Filled *with*
Assorted Sandwiches

Fresh Apple Spice Cake

Toffee Nut Bars

Wine *and* Beer *on* Ice

Montpelier, James Madison's lifelong home, was his pride, his solace, and his refuge. Built when he was five years old, it was the place he brought his vivacious bride, Dolley Payne Todd, whom he married when she was 26 and he 43. It was again to his beloved Montpelier, with its 90-mile vistas of the Blue Ridge, that he retired after his terms as president, and where he and Dolley entertained their friends with good food, wine, lively conversation, and political persuasion. His letters give a glimpse of the magnitude of their hospitality: "We had 90 persons to dine with us at our table fixed on the lawn under a large arbor." Luckily only six remained to spend the night!

After her husband's death in 1836, Dolley Madison had to sell Montpelier and most of its furnishings. She moved back to Washington where she died, impoverished, at the age of 81, not a very fitting end for one of our most intelligent and ebullient first ladies.

Montpelier changed hands six times between 1844 and 1901, when it was purchased by William duPont, Sr. He made vast alterations, inflated the house to 55 rooms and added large formal gardens. When Marian duPont Scott inherited the estate, she added a steeplechase course. A serious owner and breeder of championship racehorses, she was the first American to win the British Grand National. In 1934, she invited her neighbors

to the first Montpelier Hunt Races, an event which has been held annually in November for nearly 60 years. The National Trust for Historic Preservation inherited Montpelier from Mrs. Scott in 1984, and the proceeds from the races now go toward maintaining this significant American property.

The Montpelier Hunt Races draw thousands of people each year and are so popular that one young couple rescheduled their wedding rather than compete with it! Those who attend have earned the designation "Galloping Gourmets," for if the horse is first, food runs a close second: a tailgating competition with several categories is judged by food editors, restaurateurs, and gourmands of national standing, and the offerings are varied and elaborate, involving much thought and preparation. One group of cultural historians prepared a feast typical of the Madison era, including Jefferson's favorite recipe for chicken pie, all served with historically accurate silver and china. The wine, however, of necessity, had to be of a more recent vintage!

The "sport of kings" has been a favorite subject of both painters and sculptors, and the Virginia Museum of Fine Arts boasts many fine examples. Perhaps none captures that unrivaled panoply of color and movement better than Raoul Dufy's *Ascot* (next page). Born in Le Havre of a poor family, Dufy worked as

Raoul Dufy (French, 1877-1953), *Ascot*, ca. 1930, water-color. Collection of the Virginia Museum of Fine Arts, Richmond. Collection of Mr. and Mrs. Paul Mellon.

a clerk by day and took evening classes at the School of Fine Arts there. In 1900, on a grant of 100 francs a month from the town of Le Havre, Dufy went to Paris to study painting, and later shifted his interests to fashion and fabric design. By 1920, when he began a long stay in Vence in the south of France, his work had become brilliantly colorful, with unre-strained lines and a baroque display of curves and flourishes. The racetrack was his richest field of experiment. First he painted horses; then, spending less time on picturesque details, he started concentrating on overall impres-sions. According to one biographer, Jacques Lassaigne, "Out on the broad ribbon of track, in the bright sunlight, or in the huge shadow of the grandstand, he was naturally led to dividing the picture space into vertical stripes of blue, green, and yellow." Ascot brilliantly captures the moment — horses and riders, crowds, landscape that stretches out to the horizon — all rendered in simple outline and "drowned by the mass of ambient color."

Our tailgate picnic is a sure winner too, combining traditional Virginia foods with some surprises. Not too difficult to orches-trate, the soup travels in a sealed container to be served in a hollowed pumpkin; and the hot foods are rewarmed in an elegant double chaf-ing dish. There's a fine balance of flavors and textures: simple roasted pork tenderloin with a tangy sauce; rich, creamy hot crab; crisp veg-etables; and an assortment of sandwiches served in a bread basket. The toffee nut bars and fresh apple cake can be eaten in hand, and there is wine and beer chilled in an old copper boiler. We think the Madisons would have loved it.

PUMPKIN BISQUE

2 tablespoons margarine
½ cup finely chopped onion
½ teaspoon celery seed
2 16-ounce cans pumpkin
4 to 5 cups chicken broth, divided
2 cups half-and-half
1 tablespoon lemon juice
2 tablespoons sugar
2 ½ teaspoons salt
¼ teaspoon pepper
¼ teaspoon ground cloves
⅛ teaspoon mace
Hollowed pumpkin for serving

Melt margarine in large pan. Add onion and celery seed and cook until onion is tender but not brown. Stir in pumpkin, 4 cups broth, half-and-half, lemon juice, sugar, salt, pepper, cloves, and mace.

Bring slowly to a boil, stirring often, reduce heat and simmer 10 minutes. If too thick, add more broth for desired consistency.

Pour into hollowed pumpkin just before serving.

Serves 8

CHICKEN DRUMETTES WITH PEANUT SAUCE

1 cup sugar
½ cup vinegar
1 egg, beaten
1 tablespoon prepared mustard
1 ¼ cups crunchy peanut butter
32 chicken drumettes (unskinned)

Preheat oven to 325°.

Combine sugar, vinegar, egg, and mustard in saucepan. Simmer, stirring about 10 minutes until mixture is consistency of thin sauce. DO NOT BOIL. Remove from heat and stir in peanut butter until well blended.

Place chicken in 9 x 13-inch baking dish. Pour sauce over chicken and bake 40 minutes. May be served hot or at room temperature.

Serves 10 to 12

MARINATED PORK LOIN

1 tablespoon dry mustard
2 teaspoons dried whole thyme
½ cup soy sauce
2 cloves garlic, minced
1 teaspoon ground ginger
1 4- to 5-pound boned pork loin roast

Glaze:
1 10-ounce jar apricot preserves
1 tablespoon soy sauce
2 tablespoons dry sherry

Combine mustard, thyme, ½ cup soy sauce, garlic, and ginger, and put in plastic bag. Place roast in bag and marinate in refrigerator at least 3 to 4 hours, or as long as 2 days, turning often.

Preheat oven to 325°. Remove roast from marinade and place on rack in shallow roasting pan. Insert meat thermometer and bake until thermometer registers 155°, about 1 hour.

To make glaze, combine preserves, soy sauce, and sherry. Cook over low heat until preserves melt.

For picnics or hors d'oeuvres, slice thinly and serve with a purchased plum sauce and party rye bread.

Serves 12 to 14

FRANCES LAMBERT'S CHAFING-DISH CRAB

2 tablespoons butter
2 tablespoons flour
1 cup cream
⅛ teaspoon red pepper
⅛ teaspoon salt
⅛ teaspoon nutmeg
¼ cup sherry
2 cups lump crabmeat
Parsley for garnish

Melt butter and add flour. When it bubbles, add cream and cook until thick and smooth, stirring constantly. Stir in pepper, salt, nutmeg, and sherry. Fold in crabmeat and heat thoroughly.

Put in chafing dish and garnish with chopped parsley. Serve with toast points or in small pastry shells. May be doubled successfully.

Serves 25

MARINATED TOMATO, FETA, AND PEPPER SALAD
A tasty make-ahead salad

½ cup olive oil
2 tablespoons red wine vinegar
1 teaspoon thyme
¼ teaspoon freshly ground pepper
1 teaspoon salt
4 ounces feta cheese, crumbled
1 sweet red pepper, julienned
1 green pepper, julienned
½ pound cherry tomatoes, halved
½ cup thinly sliced red onion
½ cup sliced black olives

Mix together olive oil, vinegar, thyme, pepper, and salt. Stir in feta cheese. Pour over vegetables in serving bowl and toss. Refrigerate 6 hours or overnight.

Serves 4

FRESH APPLE SPICE CAKE

3 cups all-purpose flour
I teaspoon baking soda
I ¼ teaspoons cinnamon
¼ teaspoon ground cloves
½ teaspoon nutmeg
I teaspoon salt
2 cups sugar
3 eggs
I ½ cups vegetable oil
4 cups (about 3 large Granny Smith or
    Delicious) apples, peeled, cored, and
    coarsely chopped
I cup chopped pecans
3 tablespoons apple brandy

Topping:
  I cup whipping cream
  2 tablespoons sugar
  2 tablespoons apple brandy

Preheat oven to 325°. Spray Bundt pan with nonstick spray.

Sift together flour, soda, cinnamon, cloves, nutmeg, and salt. Stir in sugar. Beat eggs and add oil. Stir this mixture into dry ingredients. Add apples, pecans, and 3 tablespoons brandy, stirring well. Batter will be very stiff.

Spoon into pan and bake 70 minutes. Cool 10 minutes and remove from pan to cake rack. When completely cool, wrap in foil and refrigerate overnight to allow flavors to develop. Keeps well in refrigerator.

When ready to serve, whip cream, add sugar and continue beating until stiff. Stir in 2 tablespoons brandy and serve a dollop on slices of cake.

Makes 24 slices

TOFFEE NUT BARS

Bottom Layer:
  ½ cup butter
  ½ cup packed brown sugar
  I cup sifted all-purpose flour

Topping:
  2 eggs, well beaten
  I cup packed brown sugar
  I teaspoon vanilla
  2 tablespoons flour
  I teaspoon baking powder
  ½ teaspoon salt
  I cup moist shredded coconut
  I cup chopped pecans

Preheat oven to 350°.

Combine butter and sugar and mix thoroughly. Stir in flour. Press and flatten the mixture to cover the bottom of an ungreased 9 x 13-inch pan.

Bake 10 minutes.

To make topping, combine eggs, sugar, and vanilla. Mix flour, baking powder, and salt, and add to egg mixture. Add coconut and pecans. Pour mixture over bottom layer and bake 25 minutes until topping is golden brown.

Cool slightly and cut into bars.

Makes 2 ½ dozen I x 3-inch bars

MENU

Fried Chicken

Ham Loaf

Pasta *and* Mozzarella Salad

Sour Cream Potato Salad

Sweet *and* Sour Kidney Beans

Squash *with* Tomatoes *and* Cheese

Jerusalem Artichoke Pickles

Walney Indian Relish

Traditional Sally Lunn

Martha Ford's Rolls

Fresh Peach Pie

Rhubarb Crisp

Lemon Pound Cake

Blackberry Cake *with* Caramel Icing

Our biblical heritage tells us that there is a time to laugh and a time to weep, a time to sow and a time to reap, a time to be born and a time to die. And we know that all of these occasions are made more memorable and meaningful by the presence of family. Whether we gather to commiserate or to celebrate, family enhances the joy, swells the pride, and renders the grief bearable. It is the anchor for our spirit and the wind beneath our wings.

With today's mobility, indeed "globality," grandparents, parents, children, aunts, uncles, and cousins are far-flung; many live in different states and even different countries. As a result, family gatherings tend to be considerably less frequent than they were even a generation or two ago. That should make the times we are together all the more cherished and enjoyable. A family gathering should get everyone involved, especially the children. To feel included is to feel important. So share the planning, the preparation, the food. This is also a good time to gather a little family history; use a tape recorder, and depending on the occasion, prepare a list of questions for everyone to answer, especially older members. What do you remember about your childhood Christmases? What did you do on your birthdays? How did Grandmother and Grandfather meet? What was school like when you were in fourth grade, or graduating? If you transcribe

such information through the years, you will have created an invaluable treasury of family memories.

Record the occasion on videotape to relive at future gatherings. If Christmas is your special family time, use a live tree and take the family picture around it. Plant it after the holidays, and each year use it as the background for your family photograph. You'll have a record of how the tree — and the family — grows. You can even use it for next year's Christmas card. (It's good for the environment, too!)

The family gathering as a subject for art can be seen in two very different paintings in the Virginia Museum. *A Game of Skittles* by the

Queena Dillard Stovall (American, 1888-1980), *Baptizing-Pedlar River*, 1957, oil on canvas. Collection of the Virginia Museum of Fine Arts, Richmond. Gift of the artist.

18th-century Flemish artist Pieter Angellis (page 69), shows a group engaged in a game of skittles (or ninepins) outside a country inn. Others are talking beside a quiet stream. Angellis's paintings have been described as "extremely neat and prevailingly light in tone." Although not the sort of family gathering we've planned, it is a pleasant picture of happy people enjoying each other's company on a summer afternoon.

In contrast, *Baptizing at Pedlar River* by Virginia artist Queena Stovall is a simple, almost childlike, scene that can evoke both innocence and strong emotion. Stovall began painting scenes in the mountains around her native Lynchburg in 1949, when she was 61. "I went up there to see where they baptize," the artist said. "It was a pretty scene, this high rock that came up in the water, with the water running around it." In all her paintings, she comments on the beauty and brevity of life without nostalgia or sentimentality.

For our family gathering, we chose a picnic under the trees at Tuckahoe Plantation, an 18th-century house just west of Richmond that today still echoes with children's laughter, the murmured conversation of candlelight dinners, and the daily business of life. Since it's a three-generation affair and the food a joint effort, the fare is plentiful and varied, designed to appeal to both old and young, easy to prepare at home and bring along, either to be reheated or eaten cold. The luscious desserts make use of summer's bounteous fruits; make plenty — everyone will eat at least two!

Do plan your family gathering soon. It takes a lot of preparation and teamwork, but everyone will agree the rewards are worth it!

FRIED CHICKEN

**2- to 3-pound chicken, cut into
      serving pieces
Salt and pepper
¾ cup buttermilk
2 cups all-purpose flour
I teaspoon salt
½ teaspoon pepper
I to I ½ cups solid shortening**

Rinse chicken pieces and pat dry. Sprinkle
lightly with salt and pepper. Set aside 15 to 20
minutes.

Put buttermilk in bowl; add chicken and
coat thoroughly. In another bowl, combine
flour, salt, and pepper. Lightly flour each piece
of chicken.

Using a heavy 12-inch frying pan, heat
shortening to 375°. Add chicken, being careful not to cover chicken with hot grease.
Reduce heat to medium. Cover pan and brown
chicken on one side, about 12 to 15 minutes.
Turn chicken, cover pan, and continue cooking until brown. Drain on absorbent paper.

Pieter Angellis (Flemish, 1685-1734), *A Game of Skittles*, 1727, oil on canvas. Collection
of the Virginia Museum of Fine Arts, Richmond. The Paul Mellon Collection.

HAM LOAF

2 pounds ground smoked ham
2 pounds ground fresh uncooked pork
1 ½ cups fresh cracker crumbs
½ cup chopped onion
4 eggs, well beaten
1 ¼ teaspoons salt
2 cups milk
2 tablespoons fresh parsley, finely chopped

Glaze:
  ½ pound brown sugar
  ½ cup cider vinegar
  1 ½ tablespoons dry mustard

Mustard Sauce:
  ½ cup mayonnaise
  ½ cup sour cream
  ¼ cup mustard
  1 tablespoon freshly minced chives
  2 tablespoons or more horseradish

❦ Preheat oven to 350°.

❦ Combine ham and pork. Combine cracker crumbs, onion, eggs, salt, milk, and parsley. Add to meat mixture and mix thoroughly.

❦ Shape into 2 loaves and put in 2 loaf pans (9 x 5 x 3-inch). Bake 30 minutes.

❦ To make the glaze, combine sugar, vinegar, and dry mustard, and boil for 1 minute. Remove loaves from oven, baste with glaze, and bake 1 hour more. Remove loaves from pans. Freezes nicely.

❦ To make the mustard sauce, combine mayonnaise, sour cream, mustard, chives, and horseradish. Serve 1 tablespoon on each slice of ham loaf. Put remainder in a sauce boat. The sauce is a must. Freezes very nicely.

❦ Serves 20

PASTA AND MOZZARELLA SALAD

6 ounces shells or corkscrew pasta
10 ounces fresh spinach, torn in pieces
8 ounces mozzarella cheese, cubed
8 ounces country ham, thinly sliced
1 pint cherry tomatoes, halved

Parmesan dressing:
  1 egg
  1 ¾ cup salad oil
  ½ cup grated Parmesan cheese
  ¼ cup white wine vinegar
  ½ to 1 teaspoon pepper
  ½ teaspoon salt
  1 to 2 cloves garlic, minced

❦ Cook pasta according to directions, drain, rinse in cold water, and drain again. Combine pasta, spinach, mozzarella, ham, and tomatoes.

❦ To make dressing, put egg in blender, cover and blend 5 seconds. With blender running, slowly add oil until thick. Add Parmesan, vinegar, pepper, salt, and garlic. Blend until smooth.

❦ Toss salad with dressing.

❦ Serves 8

SOUR CREAM POTATO SALAD

3 pounds small new potatoes
Salt and white pepper

Dressing:
  I cup sour cream
  ½ cup mayonnaise
  ¼ cup chopped green onion
  I teaspoon Old Bay seasoning
    (or more to taste)

Boil potatoes in salted water until just tender. Drain and cut into quarters, and sprinkle with salt and pepper. Cool.

While potatoes are boiling, combine dressing ingredients to allow flavors to meld. When potatoes are cool, gently stir in dressing. Refrigerate I hour or more.

Serves 6 to 8

SWEET AND SOUR KIDNEY BEANS

6 to 8 strips bacon
4 16-ounce cans kidney beans, drained
3 large tomatoes, chopped
3 green peppers, chopped
3 onions, chopped
I cup packed dark brown sugar
I 14-ounce bottle hot ketchup

Preheat oven to 300°.

Put 3 strips bacon in bottom of 3-quart casserole. Cover with 2 cans beans. Add tomatoes, peppers, and onions. Cover with remaining beans, and sprinkle with brown sugar. Lay remaining bacon over beans and pour ketchup over all.

Bake I hour covered and I hour uncovered.

Serves 10 to 12

SQUASH WITH TOMATOES AND CHEESE

4 medium-sized yellow or zucchini squash
I ½ cups chopped onions
Butter or margarine
Nature's Seasons
Parmesan cheese
2 cups stewed tomatoes
¾ cup grated mozzarella cheese
¾ cup grated provolone cheese

Preheat oven to 350°.

Halve squash lengthwise. Boil squash and onions about 5 minutes. Drain.

Score squash and put in greased baking dish. Top with onions. Sprinkle with Nature's Seasons, then generously with Parmesan. Cover with stewed tomatoes and top generously with mixed mozzarella and provolone.

Bake until cheese melts, about I5 to 20 minutes.

Serves 8

JERUSALEM ARTICHOKE PICKLES

8 quarts Jerusalem artichokes
2 pounds sliced onions
6 pounds brown sugar
1 ¾-ounce box pickling spice
1 ⅛-ounce box celery seed
1-ounce box dry mustard
1 ¼-ounce box turmeric
1 tablespoon horseradish
2 red pepper pods
3 to 4 tablespoons salt
1 gallon apple cider vinegar

🔹 Wash artichokes thoroughly. (One good way to do this is to rinse them outside with the hose, and then put them in the washing machine on the cold water cycle.) Cut out "navel" and then into desired-size pieces. Leave small ones whole.

🔹 Mix all ingredients except artichokes and onions in large vessel and bring to a boil. Simmer while filling hot, sterilized jars with artichokes and onions. Put some onion on top.

🔹 Pour hot liquid to fill jars. Seal and keep sealed for at least 2 weeks.

🔹 Makes 16 pints

WALNEY INDIAN RELISH
Named for a lovely old Virginia house, Walney

2 cups finely chopped red sweet pepper
2 cups finely chopped green pepper
2 cups finely chopped white onions
1 large cauliflower, finely chopped
12 medium-sized cucumbers, finely chopped
¼ cup plus 2 teaspoons salt, divided
4 cups vinegar
3 ½ cups sugar
4 tablespoons mustard seed
2 teaspoons celery seed
½ teaspoon red pepper
1 teaspoon turmeric
1 teaspoon ginger
1 teaspoon alum, divided

🔹 Place peppers, onions, cauliflower, and cucumbers in large enameled kettle or bowl and cover with ¼ cup salt. Let stand overnight. Drain and rinse well.

🔹 Place vinegar, sugar, mustard seed, 2 teaspoons salt, celery seed, pepper, turmeric, and ginger in large kettle, and bring to boil. Add vegetables to boiling mixture. Bring mixture to boil again.

🔹 Pack in sterile pint jars and add ¼ teaspoon alum to each jar. Seal immediately.

🔹 Makes 4 pints

TRADITIONAL SALLY LUNN
Also excellent toasted and buttered

1 cup milk
¼ cup water
½ cup vegetable shortening
4 cups sifted flour, divided
⅓ cup sugar
2 teaspoons salt
2 packages dry yeast
3 eggs

🔹 Butter or spray a Bundt pan with nonstick cooking spray.

🔹 Heat milk, water, and shortening to 120°.

🔹 Combine 1 ⅓ cups flour with sugar, salt, and yeast in large bowl. Add warm liquid to flour mixture. Beat with electric mixer on medium speed for 2 minutes.

🔹 Add ⅔ cup flour and the eggs. Beat at high speed 2 minutes. Add 2 cups flour and mix well. Batter will be thick but not stiff.

🔹 Cover and let rise until double in bulk (about 1 ¼ hours). Punch dough down and put into prepared pan. Cover and let rise until it has increased ⅓ to ½.

🔹 Preheat oven to 350°.

🔹 Bake 40 to 50 minutes. Cool on rack.

🔹 Serves 16 to 24

MARTHA FORD'S ROLLS
A wonderfully simple classic dinner roll

¼ cup sugar
½ cup vegetable shortening
¾ teaspoon salt
½ cup boiling water
1 package dry yeast
½ cup lukewarm water (115°)
1 egg, slightly beaten
3 cups flour
Melted butter for dipping

Cream sugar, shortening, and salt. Pour ½ cup boiling water over ingredients and let cool slightly. Dissolve yeast in ½ cup lukewarm water and add to melted ingredients along with egg. Sift 3 cups flour and add to yeast mixture. Cover and refrigerate overnight.

Two hours before baking, roll out dough on floured surface and cut with 2 ½-inch round cookie cutter.

Dip into melted butter and fold over into a half-circle "pocketbook." Place on baking sheet and let rise in warm place until rolls double in size.

Preheat oven to 400° and bake about 15 minutes or until browned. May be frozen.

Makes 14 to 16

FRESH PEACH PIE

1 stick butter
1 cup powdered sugar
1 teaspoon almond extract, divided
1 9-inch pie shell, baked
8 to 10 firm, ripe peaches
Sugar to taste
½ pint whipping cream, whipped

Cream butter and powdered sugar well. Add ½ teaspoon almond extract and blend well. Smooth into cool baked pie shell and chill until mixture is firm.

Peel and slice peaches into bowl, sprinkle with sugar to taste and set aside. Just before serving, drain peaches well and pour into pie shell. Top with whipped cream slightly sweetened with sugar and flavored with remaining ½ teaspoon almond extract.

Serves 6 to 8

RHUBARB CRISP

3 cups ½-inch-cut pieces rhubarb
3 ounces strawberry or raspberry gelatin
1 ½ cups flour
1 cup quick-cooking rolled oats
1 cup or less firmly packed brown sugar
1 teaspoon cinnamon
¾ cup butter or margarine, melted

Preheat oven to 375°.

Place rhubarb in ungreased 9-inch square pan. Sprinkle with gelatin. In bowl, mix flour, oats, brown sugar, cinnamon, and butter. Spoon over rhubarb.

Bake 40 to 45 minutes. Serve warm or cold, plain or with cream or ice cream.

Serves 6 to 8

LEMON POUND CAKE

3 cups sugar
3 sticks margarine
6 eggs
3 cups all-purpose flour
1 teaspoon baking powder
1 cup milk
2 tablespoons lemon extract

Preheat oven to 325°.

Cream sugar and margarine until fluffy. Add eggs 1 at a time, beating well after each addition.

Combine flour and baking powder. Add flour mixture in thirds, alternately with milk. Stir in lemon extract.

Pour mixture into greased and floured tube pan. Bake 1 hour and 15 minutes or until a toothpick inserted into center comes out clean. Cool completely before removing from pan. Serve with your favorite ice cream, topping, or fruit.

Serves 24

BLACKBERRY CAKE

This cake was a favorite dessert at a small Virginia inn for many years.

1 ½ cups sugar
¾ cup butter
3 eggs, separated and beaten
1 teaspoon cinnamon
½ teaspoon ground cloves
½ teaspoon freshly grated nutmeg
¼ teaspoon salt
3 scant cups sifted flour
1 cup buttermilk
1 rounded teaspoon baking soda
2 tablespoons cold water
1 cup blackberry jam

Preheat oven to 375°. Grease and flour 3 9-inch round cake pans.

Cream sugar and butter, and add well-beaten egg yolks.

Sift cinnamon, cloves, nutmeg, and salt with flour. Add flour mixture and buttermilk alternately to butter mixture. Add jam.

Beat egg whites until stiff. Fold into cake batter.

Divide batter into pans and bake about 25 minutes. Frost with Caramel Icing.

Serves 14 to 16

CARAMEL ICING

1 stick butter
1 cup firmly packed light brown sugar
¼ cup evaporated milk
1 ½ cups powdered sugar
¾ cup chopped pecans

Combine butter, brown sugar, and milk. Boil 1 minute.

Remove from heat, cool to lukewarm, add powdered sugar and beat until smooth. Will cover one 2-layer cake.

If using this recipe with the Blackberry Cake, double recipe and use ½ of the icing plus ¾ cup chopped pecans for the first 2 layers. Then stack third layer on top of iced layers and ice entire cake with remaining icing, omitting pecans.

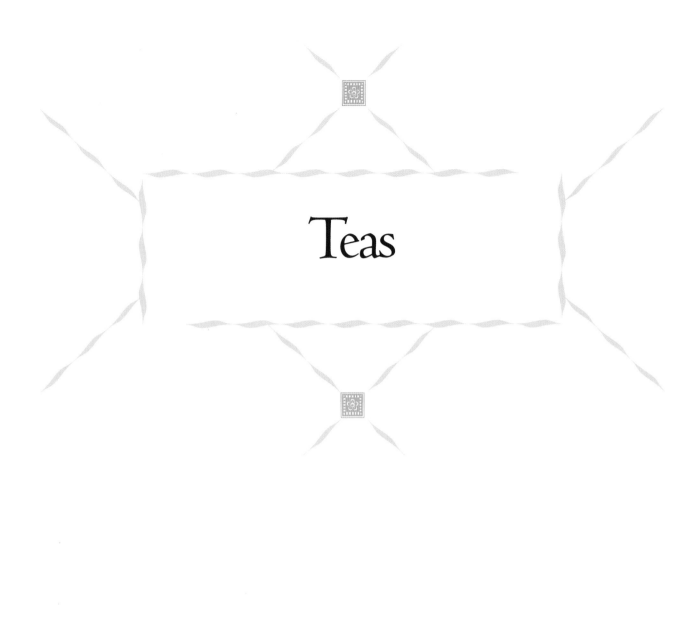

Teas

GARDEN WEEK TEA
WINCHESTER

MENU

Drop Scones

White Chocolate Almonds

Parsley Bacon Roll-ups

Cherry Tomato Rolls

Chocolate Diamonds

Tea Cookies

Iced Almond Tea

*I*n the autumn of 1928, the fledgling Garden Club of Virginia met in Fredericksburg to devise a way to raise monies to restore the gardens at Kenmore, which were in a sad state of neglect. It was proposed that private gardens throughout Virginia be opened to the public for a week in the spring, charging a small admission fee at each one. The proceeds would be used to finance the restoration of Kenmore's grounds. Visitors came, success was instant, and Historic Garden Week in Virginia was born. Little did those ladies realize how much their idea would mean to the state and to historic preservation. To date, 35 historic gardens have been authentically restored with proceeds raised from this event.

Garden Week is held annually during the third week in April when, if Mother Nature cooperates, Virginia is arguably the most glorious garden on earth — giddy with color, intoxicating with fragrance, riotous with birds and bees, and bursting with buds. No wonder hundreds of thousands of people come to view this "Ziegfield Follies" of flowers!

At the Virginia Museum, there are so many fine flower paintings that it is hard to select those that most typify Garden Week. The two shown here are both diverse and evocative.

Claude Monet's *Camille at the Window — Argenteuil* (page 79) is an early example of Impressionist painting, which featured accidental effects of light. The setting of this painting is the house Monet rented for his family from 1871 to 1874. The figure of Madame Monet, visible in the background, provides an accent for the play of light on the potted fuchsias in the foreground.

Charles Caryl Coleman's *Quince Blossoms* (next page) celebrates the artist's sophisticated sense of beauty. Coleman collected and lived with the objects in this highly formalized still life; in this case, he even designed the frame. He chose an elegant branch of flowering quince to complement the pottery and porcelains, which he placed against the delicate fabric that serves as the background. Coleman's symmetrical composition and shallow spaces were derived from Japanese art, which became ever more popular as Japan opened her shores to Western commerce in the mid-19th century. By the early 20th century, flatness and asymmetry had become hallmarks of abstract painting.

After a long spring day of viewing houses, gardens, and nature's artwork, the best place for a respite is a cool gazebo stocked with iced tea, fresh mint, and light delectables. Ours is set in Winchester, a charming small city in Virginia's northern Shenandoah Valley apple country. Winchester really has an extended garden week; surrounded by miles of apple

Charles Caryl Coleman (American, 1840-1928), *Quince Blossoms*, 1878, oil on canvas. Collection of the Virginia Museum of Fine Arts, Richmond. Museum Purchase, The J. Harwood and Louise B. Cochrane Fund for American Art.

orchards, it is the site of the annual Shenandoah Apple Blossom Festival, which has been held during the first week in May for more than six decades. The festival includes dances, a grand parade, band competitions, a national circus, and a 10-K run, and is culminated by the coronation of Queen Shenandoah, always the daughter of a national celebrity — sometimes the president, as in the case of Luci Johnson and Susan Ford. The parade alone has drawn more than 200,000 people!

The food for our tea is easy to prepare; the tea itself can be brewed in the morning, before you start garden-touring. Parsley bacon roll-ups can be prepared in quantity and frozen (a very convenient little hors d'oeuvre to have on hand), cherry tomato rolls go together in a flash, and the tea cookies and chocolate diamonds can be baked the day before. So everyone will end the day refreshed and ready for tomorrow's tour, including the hostess.

Please come and join us for the joys of Garden Week. And bring your camera, so you can capture and keep your own floral "painting."

DROP SCONES
An English approach to
morning coffee or afternoon tea

3 cups all-purpose flour
1 teaspoon baking soda
2 teaspoons baking powder
¼ teaspoon salt
½ cup sugar
¾ cup butter or margarine
½ cup raisins, chopped pecans,
   or a mixture of both
½ cup buttermilk

Preheat oven to 375°.

Sift flour, soda, baking powder, salt, and sugar. Cut in butter with 2 knives, until pea size.

Add raisins, pecans, or a mixture of both. Stir in buttermilk.

Drop on ungreased pan and bake 15 to 17 minutes.

Makes 2 dozen

WHITE CHOCOLATE ALMONDS

1 cup blanched, toasted almonds
2 1-ounce squares white coating chocolate, or enough to cover almonds
1 1-ounce square dark semisweet coating chocolate

Melt white chocolate in double boiler over hot water.

Dip almonds in melted chocolate and cool on wax paper.

Melt dark chocolate and drizzle a thin line design on each nut.

Store in covered container until ready to serve.

Claude Monet (French, 1840-1926) *Camille at the Window, Argenteuil*, 1873, oil on canvas. Collection of the Virginia Museum of Fine Arts, Richmond. Collection of Mr. and Mrs. Paul Mellon.

PARSLEY BACON ROLL-UPS

1 stick butter, softened
1 bunch fresh parsley or watercress,
    chopped
½ pound bacon, crisp cooked, drained, and
    finely crumbled
2 to 4 tablespoons mayonnaise
1 teaspoon Worcestershire sauce
1 loaf very fresh sandwich bread, crusts
    trimmed off

Cream butter. Add parsley, bacon, mayonnaise, and Worcestershire sauce. Mix to a
spreading consistency.

With rolling pin, slightly flatten each piece
of trimmed bread.

Spread parsley mixture on bread slices.

Roll slices up in wax paper, twist ends of
paper, and freeze.

To serve, unwrap and slice each roll into 4
pieces. They thaw immediately. May also be
made as square sandwiches, frozen, then sliced
into fingers or triangles.

Makes ~~9 dozen~~ 56 pieces / *Double all ingredients for whole loaf.*

CHERRY TOMATO ROLLS

12 cherry tomatoes, sliced about
    ⅛-inch thick
½ cup herbed oil and vinegar salad dressing
1 stick butter, softened
1 dozen party rolls

Marinate tomatoes in salad dressing about
30 minutes. Drain well.

Make shallow, vertical slice in top of each
roll. Spread butter on sides of cut.

Place several slices of tomato in slit so that
tomato sticks above top of roll.

Serve immediately.

Makes 1 dozen

CHOCOLATE DIAMONDS
*These are better than brownies
and just as easy to make.*

1 ounce unsweetened chocolate
¼ cup butter or margarine
½ cup sugar
1 egg
¼ cup flour
⅛ teaspoon salt
¼ teaspoon vanilla
⅓ cup chopped walnuts

Preheat oven to 375°.

Melt chocolate and butter in heavy saucepan
over very low heat.

Add sugar, egg, flour, salt, and vanilla. Mix
well.

Spread into 2 greased 8 x 8-inch pans.
Sprinkle with chopped walnuts.

Bake 10 to 12 minutes. Check corners for
burning.

Cool slightly and cut into diamonds or
squares. They will be very thin.

When cooled completely, remove carefully.
Store in airtight container. Freezes well.

Makes 4 to 5 dozen

TEA COOKIES

1 stick butter
1 stick margarine
1 ½ cups sugar
1 large egg, beaten
2 ½ cups flour
½ teaspoon baking soda
1 teaspoon cream of tartar
2 teaspoons vanilla
1 cup chopped pecans

Preheat oven to 325°.

Cream together butter, margarine, and sugar. Add egg and mix well.

Mix dry ingredients and add gradually, mixing well. Stir in vanilla and pecans.

Roll into small balls. Place on ungreased cookie sheet, and flatten with bottom of small glass dipped in sugar. A piece of pecan may be added as decoration.

Bake 12 to 15 minutes. Do not allow cookies to bake to a brown color. They should be pale golden.

Makes 5 dozen

ALMOND TEA

3 tea bags
½ cup sugar
6 cups water
Juice of 1 lemon
2 teaspoons almond extract
1 teaspoon vanilla extract

Steep tea bags and sugar in boiling water 10 minutes. Add lemon juice, almond extract, and vanilla extract.

Heat if to be served hot. May also be served over ice.

Serves 8

SPRING NEEDLEWORK EXHIBITION
WOODLAWN PLANTATION, MOUNT VERNON

MENU

Crumpets *with* Raspberry Jam

Cheese Straws

Sherried Pecans

Carrot Sandwiches

Ginger Muffins *with*
Grand Marnier Filling

Almond Stars

Lee Jelly Cake

Hot Tea

"Those dripping crumpets, I can see them now. Tiny crisp wedges of toast and piping hot, flaky scones. Sandwiches of unknown nature, mysteriously flavored and quite delectable, and that special gingerbread. Angel cake that melted in the mouth and his stodgier companion, bursting with peel and raisins."

Thus Daphne du Maurier recalled tea at Manderley in *Rebecca*. Whether you have experienced this delightful ritual elaborately or more simply in the manner of Pooh reminding Christopher Robin, "It's time for a little something," it makes for a highly civilized pause from the day's occupations, one that has been largely overlooked and ought to be revived in our busy lives.

In America's early days, tea was a most precious commodity, so precious in fact that one of our most historic and decisive events was the Boston Tea Party. The leaves were kept under lock and key. Even though drinking water was not all that it should be in our burgeoning and unsanitary cities, through most of the 18th century New York boasted a "Tea Water Pump" which would provide crystal-clear water "suitable for making tea."

The corollary of tea may have been sympathy in the celebrated play by Robert Anderson, but our tea marks an artistic occasion: the annual Spring Needlework Exhibition held each March at Woodlawn Plantation. This

gracious mansion was built by Nelly Custis Lewis on land bequeathed to her and her new husband, Major Lawrence Lewis, by her foster father, George Washington. The plantation's 2,000 acres were originally part of the Mount Vernon estate. A woman of many accomplishments, Nelly entertained often and generously, including among her guests such dignitaries as the Marquis de Lafayette. She was a talented musician and an outstanding needlewoman. Her 19th-century stitchery forms the nucleus of Woodlawn's needlework collection and the Needlework Exhibition, the oldest and largest of its kind in America. For three weeks every March, needlework from all over the country can be seen at Woodlawn. Entries must be the work of living persons and done with a hand-held, threaded needle. The entire mansion is used to exhibit the many categories of the competition, prizes are awarded, and the artistic level and workmanship are exquisite.

This exhibition celebrates and perpetuates an art that reached its zenith in the Middle Ages and the Renaissance. The Virginia Museum houses 45 tapestries from Brussels, Gobelins, and Beauvais. The one featured here, *Minerva Summoning Louis XIV to Arms,* was probably designed by Jean Baptiste Martin and was woven in Beauvais around 1684. Since tapestry weavers were subsidized by court patronage, it was only politic that the subjects be members of royalty, depicted in glorified and epic circumstances. Woven of wool, silk, and metallic thread, it is a tour de force of artistry, intricacy, and patience.

Also featured is a rare piece of needlework art, *The Rose Circle* (previous page), designed and executed by Nelly Custis Lewis, from the collection of Woodlawn Plantation.

Our tea is a rather formal one, but it makes some concessions to modernity in the lightness of the food and the ease with which it can be prepared and served. There is a pleasant balance of flavors, of sweets and nonsweets, plus a bow to tradition in the form of classic crumpets. You may wish to be authentic and serve Nelly's Ginger Cakes, which are baked every year by volunteers for Woodlawn's Needlework Exhibition, or substitute our Ginger Muffins with Grand Marnier Filling.

So polish the silver service, iron your grandmother's embroidered linens, and start baking. Whether it's tea for two or a hundred, it's one of the oldest, newest, and most gracious ways to entertain.

French (Beauvais), after a design by Jean-Baptiste Martin (French, 1659-1735). Woven at the atelier of Philippe Behagle (French, died 1704) *Minerva Summoning Louis XIV to Arms,* 1678-1735, wool, silk, silver, gold. Collection of the Virginia Museum of Fine Arts, Richmond. Bequest of Regina V. G. Millhiser.

CRUMPETS

½ cup boiling water
½ cup milk
I teaspoon sugar
I package yeast
I ¾ cups sifted flour
I teaspoon salt

Pour water, milk, sugar, and yeast into 2-quart bowl. Stir and let stand until yeast activates, about 10 to 15 minutes.

Add flour and salt to yeast mixture. Beat 3 minutes with wooden spoon. Batter should be thin. Cover and let stand in warm place to rise about 30 minutes.

Butter griddle lightly. Heat to 350° to 400° and arrange buttered crumpet rings on hot griddle. (Six-ounce tuna fish cans smoothly opened on top and bottom do the trick!) When griddle is hot, beat batter again 3 minutes. Spoon batter into rings to cover bottom just barely. Cook until surface is dry and bottom is brown. Remove rings and brown other side very lightly.

Serve warm or toasted with butter and jam.

CHEESE STRAWS

I ½ sticks butter or I stick butter
    and ½ stick margarine.
I ¾ cups all-purpose flour
8 ounces New York Aged Reserve cheese,
    grated
I teaspoon salt
⅛ teaspoon red pepper
I teaspoon paprika

Preheat oven to 350°.

Put metal blade in food processor and add butter cut into I-inch pieces. Add flour, cheese, salt, pepper, and paprika. Pulse mixture on-off 3 to 4 times to mix. Turn processor on and let run until mixture forms a ball.

Put dough in cookie press, using star-pattern disk. Press dough through cookie press onto ungreased cookie sheet. Cut into 3-inch pieces.

Bake 8 to 10 minutes, watching carefully. Do not brown.

Cool on wire rack. Store in airtight container.

SHERRIED WALNUTS OR PECANS

I ½ cups sugar
½ cup sherry
I pound shelled walnuts or pecans
Grated rind of I orange

Cook sugar and sherry to soft-ball stage on candy thermometer. Add nuts and rind. Stir until cloudy or sugary, and pour out on wax paper.

Separate into pieces with 2 forks .

CARROT SANDWICHES

I 8-ounce package cream cheese, softened
½ teaspoon dried, minced onion
¼ cup mayonnaise
½ to ¾ cup chopped carrots
I loaf thinly sliced white bread

※ Add cream cheese, onion, and mayonnaise to coarsely chopped carrots in food processor, and blend using plastic blade. Add more mayonnaise if needed to make mixture spreadable.

※ Remove crusts from bread and spread half with mixture. Top with remaining bread. Cut into finger-size sandwiches.

※ Makes 18

GINGER MUFFINS WITH GRAND MARNIER FILLING

½ cup shortening
½ cup sugar
2 eggs
I teaspoon baking soda
½ cup sour cream or buttermilk
½ cup molasses
2 cups all-purpose flour
½ teaspoon baking powder
I teaspoon ground ginger
⅛ teaspoon allspice
⅛ teaspoon cinnamon
¼ cup raisins
¼ cup chopped pecans

※ Preheat oven to 350°.

※ Cream shortening and gradually add sugar, beating until light and fluffy. Add eggs I at a time, beating well after each addition.

※ Dissolve baking soda in sour cream or buttermilk and stir into creamed mixture along with molasses. Combine flour, baking powder, ginger, allspice, cinnamon, raisins, and pecans, mixing well. Add to batter and stir just until moistened. Spoon batter into small greased muffin pans, filling half full.

※ Bake 12 to 15 minutes. Serve with Grand Marnier Filling.

※ Makes 3 dozen

GRAND MARNIER FILLING

2 8-ounce packages cream cheese, softened
Grated rind of 2 oranges
4 tablespoons Grand Marnier liqueur
4 tablespoons powdered sugar
½ to I tablespoon cream to thin
    if needed

※ Mix all ingredients. Split muffins in half and spread about I teaspoon of cheese mixture on each bottom piece. Replace tops and serve.

ALMOND STARS

1 cup butter, softened
1 ¼ cups granulated sugar
¼ teaspoon almond extract
Dash salt
1 ¼ cups finely ground, unblanched
   almonds
1 ¾ cups flour
Confectioners' sugar

Preheat oven to 325°.

Cream butter, add sugar, and beat until light. Add almond extract. Stir in salt, ground almonds, and flour.

Roll out to ⅛-inch thickness. Cut with small star cutter.

Bake 8 to 10 minutes. Remove from pan while still warm. Cool on wire rack.

Dust with sifted powdered sugar and store in airtight container. Freezes well.

Makes 10 to 12 dozen

LEE JELLY CAKE
Based on Robert E. Lee's mother's very own recipe

2 sticks butter
2 cups sugar
4 eggs
3 cups unsifted flour
1 teaspoon baking powder
½ teaspoon nutmeg
1 5-ounce can evaporated milk plus
   3 ounces water
2 teaspoons almond or vanilla extract
1 18-ounce jar strawberry preserves or any
   other red jam
Powdered sugar
3 12-inch pizza pans with ⅝-inch sides

Preheat oven to 375°. Butter pans and line with wax paper.

Cream butter and sugar and beat in eggs 1 at a time. Sift together flour, baking powder, and nutmeg, and add to creamed mixture alternately with milk and water mixture. Add extract and beat until smooth.

Divide mixture between 3 pans and bake 18 to 20 minutes, or until barely golden colored. (If you have to bake the third pan separately, check after 15 minutes.)

Cool on racks. Peel off wax paper before layers are entirely cool.

Sprinkle a little powdered sugar on large, very flat cake plate. Spread strawberry preserves or red jam between 3 layers.

Sieve powdered sugar over top of cake and cut in diamond pattern, by slicing vertically 1 inch apart. Then cut 1-inch slices on the diagonal. Do not try any other size pans — they must have ⅝" sides.

Makes 24 one-inch squares

Cocktails

A Cocktail Party

THE VIRGINIA MUSEUM OF FINE ARTS, RICHMOND

The world over, the cocktail is regarded as a uniquely American invention, almost a symbol of our way of life, but in reality, it may not be American at all. The facts of its genesis are murky, but several theories are plausible. H. L. Mencken informs us in his tongue-in-cheek analysis from *The American Language:*

1. That "cocktail" is derived from *coquetel,* the name of a mixed drink known in the vicinity of Bordeaux and introduced to America by French officers during the Revolution.

2. That it descends from *cock ale,* a mixture of ale and the essence of a boiled fowl, traced as far back as 1648 in England.

3. That in the days of cock fighting, spectators used to toast the cock with the most feathers left in its tail after the contest, the number of ingredients in the drink corresponding with the number of feathers left.

4. That the old Roosevelt Hotel in New Orleans claims the cocktail originated in that city soon after 1800, attributing it to Antoine Amédée Peychaud, the inventor of Peychaud bitters. Since he used brandy made by Sazerac du Forge et Fils of Limoges, France, his cocktails were called Sazeracs. Rye later replaced the brandy.

Regardless of the cocktail's origins, characteristic American initiative and imagination addressed itself to the creation and naming of drinks. Between the Revolution and the Civil War, many fantastic concoctions were invented, including the Eggnog (1775), the Fog-Cutter (1833), the Stone Fence, a mixture of cider and whiskey (1843), and the Black-Jack (1863). Mercifully, we have forgotten how to make most of them. The highball came in about 1898 on the heels of Scotch whisky, which was rarely drunk in America before 1895.

Whatever its etymology, the cocktail has become somewhat of a ritual in America, and the cocktail party a favorite way of entertaining. It is certainly one of the most versatile, covering everything from "a few friends over for a drink" to the most elaborate of receptions. It can be a vehicle for celebrating anything – a birthday, an anniversary, a new home, a bon voyage, an engagement, or any holiday. Its food can be as simple as vegetables with a dip or a wedge of cheese with fruit, or as elaborate as a "demi-dinner," substantial enough so that guests do not have to go in search of "real food" when they depart.

However, if it's drama you want, there can be no more spectacular setting than the Virginia Museum Sculpture Garden, where we have set our cocktail buffet. With the water splashing ecstatically over the giant limestone slabs (designed by San Francisco landscape architect Lawrence Halprin) and the late sun glowing on the trees beyond, the ambiance is cool, exciting, and sophisticated. Sharing center stage with the food is Aristide Maillol's

monolithic statue of a female nude, *La Rivière* (page 90). She reclines at the edge of the fountain, looking as if she might have just had a delightful splash.

One of the most significant international artists and sculptors of his time, Maillol turned to sculpture at age 40 because of severely impaired vision. When he first exhibited in this country in 1925, he was what historians called a classic artist, even a traditionalist. The composure of his nude bronzes reveals his personal aesthetics: "For my taste there should be as little movement as possible in sculpture." There is poise and a majestic restraint in his work, as well as perfection in the rendering of the female form. When asked why he limited himself to this subject, he replied, "Is there anything more beautiful?" In his hands, perhaps not!

We've used the glowing colors of sunset on our tables: peachy-apricot cloths, full-blown coral gladioli in a glittering mirrored cylinder, rosy shrimp stuffed with Roquefort, a crab mold surrounded by carnelian-tinted crab claws and avocado. And we've included an insidiously good caviar cake layered with whipped cream cheese, minced green scallions, and a pâté mousse, among other treats.

With cocktail parties, you can really let your imagination soar — there are so many ways to create an atmosphere and set a mood.

Looking in your attic, your china or linen closet, and your pantry can often generate ideas. A huge straw sombrero and a serape from a trip to Mexico might spark a Southwest fiesta with mini fajitas; empanadas; taco filling wrapped, for a change, in lettuce leaves; guacamole (fill the sombrero brim with blue and white corn chips); sangria — both red and white; Margaritas; and Mexican *cervesa* as well as the usual libations. Or you could expand your horizons and make a series of card tables (covered in the appropriate color of linen) into food kiosks: mini bratwurst and sausages, mustards, party pumpernickel, and rye for Germany; tiny quiches and escargots for France; smoked salmon and fresh dilled cucumbers and whole green beans (good finger-food) for Norway; glazed sliced brisket of beef and baby scones with shaved ham for England; cheese fondues with crusty bread and vegetables and chocolate fondues with fruits for Switzerland. You could even have a cocktail picnic, packing each couple's hors d'oeuvres and drinks and/or wine in individual baskets for enjoying in a meadow, under a tree, or around the pool. At any party, it is both thoughtful and sensible to have a table near the door with demitasse and cookies for your guests before they leave.

Cocktail parties can have cachet and expansiveness of a sort that — if they are done well — no other form of entertaining has.

With tongue in cheek, Ogden Nash attempted to capture that indefinable "something" in his poem entitled "A Drink with Something in It."

> *There is something about an old-fashioned*
> *That kindles a cardiac glow;*
> *It is soothing and soft and impassioned*
> *As a lyric by Swinburne or Poe.*
> *There is something about an old-fashioned*
> *When dusk has enveloped the sky,*
> *And it may be the ice,*
> *Or the pineapple slice;*
> *But I strongly suspect it's the rye.*

MOBJACK BAY CRAB MOLD

8 ounces fresh crabmeat, well shredded
8 ounces cream cheese, softened
1 stick butter
1 teaspoon capers, minced
¾ cup finely chopped celery
1 small onion, minced or grated
3 tablespoons lemon juice
1 teaspoon Worcestershire sauce
1 teaspoon Old Bay seasoning
2 tablespoons mayonnaise
2 dashes hot pepper sauce
Salt and pepper to taste

⊠ Mix all ingredients well and season with salt and pepper.

⊠ Pour into 3-cup mold and refrigerate 3 to 4 hours. Unmold on serving platter and garnish as desired.

⊠ Yields 3 cups

CAVIAR CAKE

2 8-ounce packages cream cheese, divided
1 ½ cups grated onion, divided
Dash salt
Mayonnaise
8 ounces liverwurst
Dash hot pepper sauce
Several dashes Worcestershire sauce
2 tablespoons horseradish
Salt and pepper to taste
1 3 ½-ounce jar red or black caviar

⊠ Combine 8 ounces cream cheese, ½ cup onion, dash salt, and enough mayonnaise to make mixture smooth. Roll into ball and flatten on serving plate.

⊠ Combine liverwurst, ½ cup onion, hot pepper sauce, Worcestershire sauce, horseradish, and salt and pepper.

⊠ Roll into ball and flatten. Place over cream cheese layer.

⊠ Repeat cream cheese layer and place on top of middle layer.

⊠ Refrigerate 1 day.

⊠ Spread caviar on top (with as little juice as possible) when ready to serve.

⊠ Serve with crackers. Serves 30 to 35

SEABREEZE SCALLOPS

1 pound scallops (bay or sea)
2 teaspoons Old Bay seasoning
2 cups boiling water
¾ cup lime juice
2 scallions, chopped
3 tablespoons olive oil
¾ teaspoons salt
½ teaspoon pepper
¼ cup chopped parsley
Small (3 ½-ounce) jar red caviar

⊠ Bring water and Old Bay seasoning to a boil in a saucepan. Rinse scallops and place in boiling water. Allow to cook about four minutes. Remove from heat and immediately submerge the scallops in a bowl of ice water for four to five minutes until completely cold. Pat dry with a paper towel. Place scallops in a glass container.

⊠ Mix lime juice, scallions, olive oil, salt, and pepper, and pour over scallops. Store in refrigerator overnight.

⊠ At serving time, drain and add parsley.

⊠ May also be served on lettuce and garnished with red caviar.

⊠ Serves 4 as a main dish, many more for cocktails

MARINATED
LEG OF LAMB FILLETS
WITH MINT SAUCE

I 5-pound leg of lamb, boned
I garlic clove, minced
½ teaspoon ground pepper
¼ teaspoon thyme
¼ teaspoon marjoram
¼ teaspoon oregano
I teaspoon Worcestershire sauce
¼ cup olive oil
I cup dry red wine
I medium onion, sliced

Mint Sauce:
⅓ cup mayonnaise
⅔ cup mint jelly

Place lamb in deep glass container. In small bowl, combine garlic, pepper, thyme, marjoram, oregano, Worcestershire sauce, olive oil, wine, and onion. Pour over lamb and marinate in refrigerator several hours or overnight, turning frequently.

Preheat oven to 350°.

Remove from marinade. Roast uncovered until desired degree of doneness, 125° to 130° for medium rare. Chill and cut in thin slices. Serve with cocktail breads and Mint Sauce.

For Mint Sauce, mix mayonnaise and mint jelly together and blend well.

Serves 24

ANNE'S BRIE

I baby Brie, 6 to 8 inches in diameter
I bottle Major Grey's Chutney, chopped
   in food processor
6 slices bacon, fried and crumbled, or
   bacon bits to cover top of cheese

Preheat oven to 350°.

Remove top skin from Brie. Spread chutney over top to cover. Sprinkle with bacon to cover.

Bake 5 to 7 minutes or until soft and slightly runny. Serve with crackers.

Serves 10 to 12

HAM BUTTER
IN CYMLIN SQUASH

½ cup sweet butter, softened
I cup ground smoked ham
I cymlin squash, hollowed

Beat butter and ham until they form a smooth paste. Pack into a hollowed-out cymlin squash and serve with Angel Biscuits.

Yields I cup

ANGEL BISCUITS

1 package dry yeast
2 tablespoons warm water
5 cups flour
1 teaspoon salt
1 teaspoon baking soda
1 tablespoon baking powder
¼ cup sugar
1 cup vegetable shortening
2 cup buttermilk
Melted butter

Preheat oven to 400°.

Dissolve yeast in water and set aside.

Sift together flour, salt, baking soda, baking powder, and sugar. Cut in shortening.

Add yeast mixture and buttermilk. Knead enough to hold together.

Roll out dough to ½-inch thickness on a floured surface. Cut with 2-inch biscuit cutter, fold in half, brush with butter, and bake 12 to 15 minutes.

Dough may be frozen and used as needed. It keeps in refrigerator unfrozen about 1 week. Baked biscuits may also be frozen.

Makes 20 to 25

CHEESE MOLD WITH FRUIT

½ cup golden raisins
Almond liqueur to cover
4 3-ounce packages cream cheese, softened
½ cup butter, softened
½ cup yogurt at room temperature
1 tablespoon unflavored gelatin
¼ cup cold water
½ cup sugar
Grated rind of 2 lemons
1 cup toasted, slivered almonds, divided
Assorted fruit: kiwi, strawberries, grapes, etc.

Soak raisins in almond liqueur 30 minutes.

Mix cream cheese, butter, and yogurt until smooth.

Soften gelatin in ¼ cup cold water and dissolve with sugar in double boiler over boiling water. When dissolved, cool and add to cheese mixture. Blend in raisins and remaining liqueur, lemon rind, and part of almonds, saving some for garnish.

Spray 9-inch pan or mold with nonstick cooking spray. Pour mixture into mold and refrigerate overnight.

Unmold and decorate with assorted fruits and almonds. Serve with crackers.

Serves 50 to 60

STUFFED SHRIMP

2 quarts salted water
24 unshelled large shrimp
3 ounces cream cheese
1 ounce blue cheese or Roquefort
½ teaspoon prepared mustard
1 teaspoon finely chopped scallions
1 cup finely chopped parsley

Bring salted water to a boil, add shrimp, bring back to boil, and simmer 3 to 5 minutes.

Drain shrimp, remove shells, and devein. Split shrimp down spine about halfway through. Chill.

Meanwhile, blend cheeses, mustard, and scallions. Using a knife or small spatula, stuff cheese mixture into split backs of shrimp. Roll stuffed side of shrimp in parsley and chill again.

Makes 24

Mushroom Mousse

½ pound mushrooms, chopped
1 tablespoon butter, more if needed
1 ½ teaspoons gelatin
2 tablespoons dry sherry
¼ cup cold chicken broth
1 egg, separated
3 to 4 drops Tabasco
1 teaspoon capers, drained
2 tablespoons chopped onion
1 tablespoon lemon juice
¼ teaspoon garlic salt
⅛ teaspoon white pepper
¼ cup mayonnaise
½ cup heavy cream

Brown mushrooms in butter in large skillet. Set aside. Soften gelatin in sherry and chicken broth in electric blender for 1 to 2 minutes. Blend briefly. Add mushrooms, egg yolk, Tabasco sauce, capers, onion, lemon juice, garlic salt, white pepper, and mayonnaise. Blend until smooth. Add cream and blend again.

In small bowl, beat egg whites until stiff but not dry. Fold into mushroom mixture. Pour into lightly oiled mold and refrigerate until ready to serve.

Unmold and serve with Melba toast, plain wafers, or toast points; or spoon into poached mushroom caps, artichoke bottoms, or hollowed-out cherry tomatoes.

Makes 2 to 3 dozen

Frances Lambert's Cheese Dreams

1 pound grated *sharp* cheddar cheese (no substitutions)
1 pound soft margarine
18 hot dog rolls

Preheat broiler.

Cream grated cheese and margarine until fluffy. Chill slightly. Do not let mixture get too firm.

Slice hot dog bun horizontally, then cut each half into 4 pieces.

Spread mixture on top and sides of each slice.

Broil until golden brown. Serve immediately. Can be made 1 day ahead and refrigerated. Freezes well.

Makes 144 pieces

Brunswick Stew

1 5-pound pork shoulder roast
1 5-pound chicken
1 onion
1 carrot
1 rib celery
2 tablespoons salt, divided
4 teaspoons black pepper
2 tablespoons Worcestershire sauce
1 teaspoon Tabasco sauce
2 28-ounce cans tomatoes
1 14-ounce bottle ketchup
2 large onions, chopped
2 15-ounce cans whole kernel corn
4 cups butter beans
1 stick butter
⅓ cup lemon juice

Preheat oven to 350°.

Bake pork roast in open pan until meat can be pulled off bone. Cut into small pieces.

Boil chicken in water to cover with onion, carrot, celery, and 1 teaspoon salt. Remove meat from bones and cut into small pieces. Strain chicken stock and add pepper, Worcestershire sauce, Tabasco sauce, remaining salt, tomatoes, ketchup, onions, corn, butter beans, and chopped meats. Cook on low heat, covered, about 3 hours. When ready to serve, add butter and lemon juice.

Makes 40 cocktail or 12 to 14 single-serving one-dish meals

Dinners

OLD FIDDLERS' CONVENTION

GALAX

MENU

Hot Vidalia Onion Dip *with* Toast Points

Quick Lemon Chicken Breasts

Southern Green Beans *with* New Potatoes

Whiskey Corn Pudding

Impatient Yankee Whole-Wheat Bread

Tomato Salad

Chess Pie

For the good are always the merry
Save by an evil chance.
And the merry love the fiddle
And the merry love to dance:
And when the folk there spy me
They will all come up to me,
With "Here is the fiddler of Dooney!"
And dance like a wave of the sea.

William Butler Yeats's "Fiddler of Dooney" comes to life every year in the small town of Galax, Virginia. Held in the palm of the mountains, the town derives its name (and much of its fame) as the source of the galax leaf, an evergreen native to the southern crest of the Blue Ridge Mountains and a favored natural material of florists everywhere. But Galax is also famous for a unique artistic tradition; for more than 50 years, around the second week in August, lovers of country and mountain music have arrived in droves for the annual Old Fiddlers' Convention. Most of the people don't play music, they come just for the listening. Several hundred do come with instruments, however, to demonstrate their skills and compete for prizes in playing fiddle, guitar, mandolin, banjo, and dulcimer, just to name a few. There's also clogging (a form of dancing that combines elements of the Scottish reel and the Irish jig) and good old American bluegrass music. Contestants may use only authentic folk songs and instrumentals from the public domain. No copyrighted music is permitted.

The Old Fiddlers' Convention, which goes on for four days and is held in the local park, has become so popular that the byword is "come early!" Otherwise, it's "standing room only" for latecomers.

After a long afternoon of fiddling, banjo-picking, and toe-tapping in Galax, the tradition is food, and lots of it! Our early country dinner before the evening's competition is set under cool trees beyond the lawn. Yours could be on the front porch, out on the deck, or in a summerhouse. It features everyone's Southern favorites: Vidalia onions, lemony chicken, whiskey corn pudding, and (a bow to our New England brethren) Impatient Yankee bread. With playful country pottery, an old quilt from the attic, baskets for bread and field flowers for color, it's a meal to please hungry fiddlers everywhere from Dooney to Galax, and all who appreciate the verve and vitality of their music.

The fiddle and its family of related instruments find their derivations in the viol, developed and perfected in the Middle Ages and the Renaissance. Older still is the harp, which dates back to biblical times or even earlier in cultures throughout the world. The harp shown here, from the Mangbetu culture in Zaire, is from the Virginia Museum's fine collection of African art. Whether it is held out, fiddle-style, or placed on the ground for a squatting performer, this harp's elegant lines and snakeskin covering harmonize with the woman's head carved at the top.

Mangbetu (Zaire), *Harp*, 19th-20th century, wood, reptile skin, gut, glass beads, string. Collection of the Virginia Museum of Fine Arts, Richmond. Museum Purchase, The Kathleen Boone Samuels Memorial Fund.

HOT VIDALIA ONION DIP

I cup mayonnaise
I cup grated Swiss cheese
I cup grated Vidalia or sweet onions
Salt to taste
Juice of ½ lemon or I tablespoon
Few drops Tabasco sauce

Preheat oven to 325°.

Mix all ingredients and put into small baking dish, preferably one in which you intend to serve dip.

Bake about 15 minutes or until bubbly.

Brown top of dip under broiler about 2 minutes, watching carefully.

Serve with toast points or crackers.

Makes approximately 2 cups

QUICK LEMON CHICKEN BREASTS

2 whole boneless chicken breasts, skinned
    and cut into 4 pieces
I teaspoon dried tarragon
I teaspoon lemon juice
Pepper to taste
¼ cup Dijon mustard
I lemon, sliced
I tablespoon chopped parsley

Preheat broiler to 500°.

Flatten chicken breasts by placing meat between 2 sheets of wax paper and pounding with mallet or rolling pin.

Mix tarragon, lemon juice, pepper, and mustard. Coat chicken pieces with mixture.

Broil 4 inches from heat source until mustard coating bubbles, about 5 to 6 minutes. Turn and broil other side 5 to 6 minutes.

Top each serving with I lemon slice and chopped parsley.

Serves 4

SOUTHERN GREEN BEANS WITH NEW POTATOES

I quart (about I ½ pounds) snapped
    green beans
¼ pound bacon or I small ham hock
6 to 8 small potatoes

Wash, string, and snap beans. Put in large saucepan and cover with boiling water.

Add bacon or hock and bring to boil. Reduce heat and allow to simmer, never boil, uncovered 1 hour.

Add scrubbed potatoes and continue cooking until potatoes are done. Remove potatoes and continue simmering until liquid is reduced to approximately I cup.

Return potatoes and reheat before serving.

Serves 6

Whiskey Corn Pudding

1 10-ounce package frozen corn
1 tablespoon cornstarch
1 tablespoon sugar
¼ teaspoon salt
⅛ teaspoon freshly ground pepper
1 cup milk
3 tablespoons butter
1 ½ tablespoons bourbon whiskey
1 egg
Paprika

▦ Preheat oven to 350°.

▦ Cook corn according to directions on package. Drain and set aside.

▦ Mix together cornstarch, sugar, salt, and pepper in saucepan.

▦ Add milk gradually, stirring until smooth. Cook over medium heat, stirring constantly until thick.

▦ Remove from heat, add drained corn, butter, and whiskey.

▦ Beat egg well. Fold into corn mixture. Pour into buttered 1-quart casserole. Sprinkle with paprika.

▦ Bake 45 minutes.

▦ Serves 6 to 8

Impatient Yankee Whole-Wheat Bread
Keep the dough warm to shorten the rising time.

2 packages dry yeast
¾ cup warm water (115°)
1 ¼ cups buttermilk, heated to 100° to 110°
¼ cup shortening
2 ½ cups whole-wheat flour
3 tablespoons brown sugar
2 teaspoons salt
2 teaspoons baking soda
2 tablespoons caraway seeds (optional)
2 ½ cups all-purpose flour
3 tablespoons melted butter, divided

▦ While yeast is dissolving in warm water in large bowl, heat buttermilk and melt shortening.

▦ Once yeast is dissolved, add buttermilk, whole-wheat flour, sugar, salt, and baking soda, and slowly and *patiently* mix with electric mixer 2 minutes while adding shortening. Add caraway seeds if desired.

▦ Increase speed to medium and beat 2 minutes more. Add white flour and mix until a firm but sticky dough forms.

▦ Knead on floured board 10 minutes. Dough should still be slightly sticky. Cover dough with warm towel and let rise 10 minutes. If *impatient*, use this time to clean up.

▦ Roll out dough to 9 x 12 inches, and roll up jelly-roll fashion from short end. Seal seam, turn ends under, and place seam side down in greased loaf pan.

▦ Brush with melted butter, cover, and let rise until double in size, about 45 minutes.

▦ Preheat oven to 425°.

▦ Bake 20 minutes. Bread is done when it sounds hollow when thumped.

▦ Remove from oven and brush with rest of butter. Cool on rack.

▦ Makes 1 loaf

TOMATO SALAD

I clove garlic, halved
6 large tomatoes
I large purple onion or Vidalia sweet onion
I large green pepper
Sugar, salt, pepper, and garlic powder
   to taste
Juice of 2 lemons
2 tablespoons olive oil

Rub large dish with cut sides of garlic clove.

Peel and slice tomatoes in very thick slices.
Place in single layer in dish.

Dice onion and green pepper and sprinkle
over tomato slices.

Sprinkle tomatoes liberally with sugar, salt,
pepper, and garlic powder.

Combine lemon juice and olive oil. Drizzle
over entire dish.

Refrigerate at least 3 hours. Liquids may be
spooned over dish once or twice.

Arrange on large platter or on individual
salad plates with 2 slices served on lettuce or
greens of your choice.

Serves 6 to 8

CHESS PIE

I 9-inch unbaked pie crust
I stick butter
I cup sugar
I teaspoon cornmeal
3 eggs
5 tablespoons heavy cream
I teaspoon vanilla
I teaspoon vinegar

Preheat oven to 400°.

Put pie shell in oven and brown lightly,
about 10 to 12 minutes. Remove and cool.

Cream butter and sugar. Add cornmeal,
then I egg at a time, beating after each addition.

Add cream, vanilla, and vinegar.

Pour mixture into pie shell and bake 10
minutes at 400°; reduce to 325° and bake
45 minutes, or until set.

Serve slightly warm. Freezes well.

Makes I pie

CHINESE NEW YEAR

MENU

Five Treasure Stir-Fry

Won Ton Soup

Dancing Shrimp

Barbequed Spareribs

Green *and* White Jade

Sliced Beef *and* Broccoli

Steamed Rice

Ginger Blossom Ice Cream

*A*mong the world's cultures, China ranks as one of the highest in the arts, and in the sophistication of its symbolism and ritual. Naturally, all of these are reflected in its artful cuisine (which its devotees claim is the most innovative and delicious in the world). Of all its myriad celebrations and commemorations, the Chinese New Year is the most recognized and most widely celebrated in Western countries.

In China, on the first day of the lunar calendar, particular foods are served as much for their symbolism as for their taste. The New Year season is essentially a fresh slate, a period of renewal, a time of communal interaction among families and friends, and a time of forgiveness for wrongs and debts, when food takes on a meaning far beyond its taste and smells.

Rice is always served. It is the elemental grain, the grain of subsistence. Dates and fresh fruits signify abundance. Green is the color of jade and the symbol of youth (both much coveted), so a green vegetable, usually broccoli, always makes its way to the table. And since the first day of the lunar year also marks the first day of spring, the variety of foods indicates abundance and thanks to the God of Good Fortune, Choi Sun Doh, and, it goes without saying, to Tsao Chun, the Kitchen

God. Who else keeps the ginger fresh and the oil from burning?

Our menu for this festive oriental holiday includes many of the required foods, adapted for American tastes, yet with enough authenticity and variety to celebrate the moment with respect to its origins. (A strict Buddhist menu, however, would contain no meat.) This menu involves a fair amount of preparation time, but the results are worth it. In the true spirit of the day, it could be a joint effort of two or three hosts and hostesses!

Although the traditional decor would include an altar laden with the propitious foods, fruits, and sweets to honor both gods and guests, ours features one of the most impressive pieces in the Virginia Museum's collection of Asiatic art.

The splendid *Theatrical Robe* (next page) was made by an unknown artist in the 18th century. Fashioned of glowing embroidered satin, velvet, and silk brocade, afire with pieces of glass set in gilded metal mounts, such a fine garment could only have been meant to be worn by the star of the show. In classical Chinese theater, there are four principal groups of actors, each wearing very stylized costumes which allow the audience to recognize the special position and nature of the character being played. This robe is for a warrior character.

Chinese, Qing Dynasty (1644-1911), *Theatrical Robe*, 18th century, embroidered satin and velvet, silk brocade, glass in gilded metal mounts. Collection of the Virginia Museum of Fine Arts, Richmond. Gift of Alan Priest.

FIVE TREASURE STIR-FRY

⅓ cup bottled stir-fry sauce
1 large clove garlic, pressed
2 tablespoons vegetable oil
½ pound fresh asparagus, cut in
    2-inch pieces
1 medium onion, sliced
½ pound snow peas
1 large red bell pepper, cut in
    ½-inch strips
12 ears canned baby corn, rinsed

◼ Mix stir-fry sauce with garlic.

◼ Heat oil in wok. Add asparagus and onion and stir-fry 2 minutes. Add snow peas and stir-fry 2 minutes. Add red pepper strips and stir-fry 2 minutes. Add corn and stir-fry 1 minute. Pour in stir-fry sauce mixture and cook, stirring, until vegetables are coated.

◼ Serves 6

The gold threads are woven to simulate the chain armor worn by warriors; the jagged, vari-colored brocade borders suggest tiger claws. In contrast to the costumes, stage props were very simple, usually only a few tables and chairs set in different arrangements to represent a prison, a gate, a tower, a high mountain, and so on. This is still the custom in Chinese theater today.

From that you can take your cue for your own Chinese New Year table setting: use your imagination! A length of brocade or an oriental-design remnant from a fabric shop, paper dragons, a Canton bowl filled with pomegranates, dates, and nuts, tiny orange trees from the local nursery, arrangements of bamboo or flowering quince, a pair of ceramic pandas, or a collection of cloisonné boxes would all help set the stage for a marvelous meal. Put a length of sugarcane (a traditional Chinese sweet) at each place with the guest's name written on it instead of a place card.

And if you are lucky enough to have a fortune-cookie factory in your city, or are good friends with the owner of your local Chinese restaurant, have your invitations put inside the cookies and mail them to your guests in tiny boxes.

Ho ho Sik! (Good eating!)

WON TON SOUP

¼ pound ground pork
4 tablespoons chopped green onion, divided
I teaspoon minced fresh ginger root
2 teaspoons soy sauce
2 tablespoons vegetable oil, divided
2 tablespoons sherry, divided
I ½ teaspoons salt, divided
¾ teaspoon sugar, divided
I small egg
Dash pepper
⅓ cup finely chopped spinach
2 ounces shrimp, cleaned and chopped
I package won ton skins
2 cans chicken broth plus I cup water
6 teaspoons sesame oil
2 tablespoons shredded bamboo shoots
    or I ¼ cups thinly sliced cucumber

To make won ton filling, mix pork with 2 tablespoons green onion, ginger root, soy sauce, I tablespoon vegetable oil, I tablespoon sherry, I teaspoon salt, ½ teaspoon sugar, egg, and dash pepper.

Drain excess water out of spinach by squeezing between palms of hand. Add to pork mixture and mix well.

Marinate shrimp with I tablespoon sherry, ½ teaspoon salt, and ¼ teaspoon sugar. Add to pork mixture and mix well. Won ton filling can be refrigerated overnight or frozen.

To assemble, place ½ teaspoon filling in center of won ton skin and fold according to package directions.

In 6 cups boiling water, place 15 to 20 won tons. Add I cup cold water and bring to a boil again. Won tons are done when they float on the surface of the water.

Bring chicken broth and water to a boil. Remove won tons from water with slotted spoon and add to broth.

To serve, garnish each serving with I teaspoon sesame oil and chopped green onion, shredded bamboo shoots, or sliced cucumber. Serve hot.

Serves 6

DANCING SHRIMP

I pound shrimp, shelled and deveined
I teaspoon cornstarch
½ egg white
2 teaspoons sherry
¼ teaspoon sugar
¼ teaspoon salt
Oil for frying
I green onion, green part included,
    trimmed and cut into I-inch pieces

Rinse and dry shrimp and place in bowl. Add cornstarch and egg white and refrigerate 45 minutes.

Mix sherry, sugar, and salt, and set aside.

In a wok or deep pan, heat oil to hot. Add shrimp and stir to separate. Cook until shrimp are pink, I to 2 minutes. Drain on paper.

In same pan, add green onion, and cook a few seconds, stirring to heat.

Add sherry mixture, tossing and stirring shrimp and onions. Cook 30 seconds longer. Serve immediately.

Serves 4

Barbequed Spareribs

1 2- to 2 ½-pound rack spareribs
¼ cup soy sauce
2 tablespoons vinegar
3 tablespoons sherry or white wine
1 teaspoon finely chopped garlic
1 teaspoon grated fresh ginger
1 tablespoon sugar
3 tablespoons hoisin sauce
½ teaspoon red food coloring or
    2 tablespoons Chinese barbecue sauce
3 tablespoons honey for basting

▨ Trim fat from ribs. Place in shallow dish. Combine soy sauce, vinegar, sherry, garlic, ginger, sugar, hoisin sauce, and food coloring. Pour over ribs and marinate at room temperature 3 to 5 hours, or overnight in refrigerator.

▨ Preheat oven to 375°. Fill large roasting pan half full with water. This will catch the drips from the ribs, as well as keep them moist. Place on lowest rack of oven. Insert 3 or 4 curtain hooks (or S-shaped hooks) at each end of rack of spareribs. Hook free ends over bottom of uppermost shelf of oven, suspending ribs directly over pan of water. Roast ribs 45 minutes at 375°, then turn up heat to 450° and roast 20 to 25 minutes, or until ribs turn golden-reddish brown. Carefully remove from oven and brush with honey. Serve with kumquat barbecue sauce or plum sauce. To reheat, wrap in foil.

▨ Serves 6

Green and White Jade

2 whole chicken breasts, boned and skinned
    (about 14 ounces)
2 teaspoons salt, divided
2 tablespoons sherry
5 teaspoons cornstarch, divided
½ small egg white (use other ½ in following
    recipe)
6 tablespoons vegetable oil, divided
6 ounces pea pods, fresh or frozen
1 4-ounce can button or sliced mushrooms,
    reserving juice
2 ounces water chestnuts, sliced
1 teaspoon sugar, divided
Several dashes monosodium glutamate
2 cloves garlic, minced
¾ cup plus 2 tablespoons water, divided
1 teaspoon soy sauce

▨ Slice chicken very thin. This is easier if partially frozen. Mix well with 1 ½ teaspoons salt, sherry, 2 teaspoons cornstarch, and egg white. Let marinate while preparing next step.
In 12-inch frying pan or wok, heat 3 tablespoons oil over high heat and sauté pea pods, mushrooms, and water chestnuts. Add ½ teaspoon salt, ½ teaspoon sugar, and dash monosodium glutamate, and stir-fry 1 to 2 minutes. Remove from pan to bowl.

▨ Heat 3 more tablespoons oil in same pan over high heat, and sauté garlic for a few seconds. Add marinated chicken mixture and continue cooking until chicken turns white.

▨ Return vegetables to chicken pan and toss together 30 seconds. Remove to serving dish.

▨ In same pan, heat ¾ cup water and add reserved mushroom liquid, soy sauce, ½ teaspoon sugar, dash monosodium glutamate, and 1 tablespoon cornstarch mixed with 2 tablespoons water. Cook over medium-high heat until thickened.

▨ Pour over chicken and vegetables on serving dish and serve hot.

▨ Makes 6 to 8 side-dish or 2 to 3 main-course servings

SLICED BEEF AND BROCCOLI

1 pound flank steak, very cold or slightly
    frozen
2 tablespoons white wine
2 tablespoons soy sauce, divided
1 ½ teaspoons sugar, divided
1 teaspoon freshly chopped ginger
1 pound fresh broccoli
6 tablespoons vegetable oil, divided
1 teaspoon salt (optional)
Dash monosodium glutamate
1 ½ tablespoons cornstarch
1 green onion, chopped
1 tablespoon sesame oil

▨ Slice beef across grain, ⅛-inch thick, then
cut each slice into a 1 x 2-inch piece. If meat is
very cold, it slices more easily.

▨ Marinate at least 30 minutes, or overnight
in mixture of wine, 1 tablespoon soy sauce, 1
teaspoon sugar, and ginger. Do not substitute
powdered ginger.

▨ Wash broccoli and peel stems. Cut florets
into bite-size pieces. Slice stems diagonally
about ⅛-inch thick.

▨ Cook broccoli in boiling water 1 minute.
Drain and refrigerate.

▨ Heat 3 tablespoons oil over high heat. Stir-
fry broccoli 2 minutes, add 1 teaspoon salt, if
desired, ½ teaspoon sugar, and dash
monosodium glutamate. Remove from pan
and set aside.

▨ Coat beef with cornstarch. Heat 3 tablespoons oil in same pan and sauté onions 30
seconds. Add beef, 1 tablespoon soy sauce,
and sesame oil. Stir-fry over high heat 1 ½ to
2 minutes. Do not overcook beef.

▨ Add broccoli to beef and mix quickly.

▨ Serves 6

GINGER BLOSSOM ICE CREAM

½ cup water
¾ cup sugar, divided
7 tea bags
Ginger root to make 1 tablespoon
    ginger juice
2 eggs
1 cup milk
2 cups whipping cream
Toasted almonds for garnish (optional)
Slivered candied ginger for garnish
    (optional)

▨ Mix water with ½ cup sugar in saucepan
and bring to a boil, dissolving sugar.

▨ Remove from heat and add tea bags and
ginger juice made by finely chopping ginger
root in processor. Chill.

▨ Beat eggs with ¼ cup sugar until thick and
creamy. Cook egg mixture and milk together
over low heat, stirring constantly, until it coats
spoon. Add cream and cold tea mixture. Chill
thoroughly and freeze.

▨ To serve, top with toasted almonds or slivered candied ginger.

▨ Makes 1 quart

INTERNATIONAL AZALEA FESTIVAL

NORFOLK

AMBASSADOR'S DINNER MENU

Red Pepper Soup *with* Crème Fraîche

Melba Toast

Scallops *with* Mushrooms *in* Shells

Three-Fruit Sorbet

Swedish Veal Rollettes

Parsnips *and* Celery

Boston Lettuce *and* Watercress
with Club French Dressing

Hard Rolls *with* Sweet Butter

Cassis Ice Cream *with* Candied Violets
in Chocolate Cups

Demitasse

*I*f there is one true harbinger of spring in Virginia, we would have to say that it's the azalea. This sprightly green shrub with its clouds of blooms in both soft and brilliant hues blankets gardens, parks, and woods across the state with explosions of color .

Being festive by nature, we have to celebrate the azalea. Norfolk's International Azalea Festival is held annually to honor that city's role as headquarters for NATO's Supreme Allied Command Atlantic. A four-day celebration in April, it pays tribute to a different country of the NATO Alliance each year. Spain, the newest NATO member, was 1992's honored nation. A queen and 15 princesses selected from each of the NATO countries reign over the festivities, which include a Grand Parade, a coronation ceremony at Norfolk's magnificent Botanical Gardens, a Queen's Ball, and a spectacular air show. Musical artists and cultural displays from the honored nation are also featured.

Among the many portraits at the Virginia Museum, Francisco Goya's *General Nicolas Guye* (next page) captures the essence of military color and pomp. This portrait, executed in 1810 during the French domination of Spain, typifies Goya's commissioned works in its formality and directness. General Guye is obviously someone to be reckoned with, but he is also likable. On a base of earth tones and other dark colors, Goya applied dazzling highlights in brilliant colors to lend vitality and depth to his subject. A rapport between painter and sitter is apparent, for Guye, despite his stiff dress uniform, looks intently and with seeming interest at both his portraitist and his viewers. His tousled brown hair and animated mouth add to the immediacy of the work and render General Guye quite human and appealing. This must have been a very expensive commission, relatively speaking: according to tradition, the price of a portrait was substantially increased if the subject wished his hands shown because this would require the use of more canvas and more paint.

There is no better excuse for a formal dinner than a visit from an ambassador, which occurs yearly at the Azalea Festival. We have set our Ambassador's Dinner in the most elegant of oval dining rooms decorated with luxurious linens, lots of candlelight, and a centerpiece of azaleas, of course! A fleet admiral's own china, its glowing cobalt blue with gold stars a rich counterpoint to the patina of silver and the flash of crystal, is the perfect receptacle for seven courses of elegant food. Red pepper soup is a bright counterpoint to the tender, creamy scallops and the delicate veal rollettes enhanced by the earthy zip of root vegetables. The denouement is a refreshingly tart cassis ice cream served in a chocolate cup, topped with a dollop of whipped cream and a candied violet to create a lovely palette of colors.

Formal dinners are admittedly a bit of an effort, but certain occasions call for nothing less. They do give you a chance to display your loveliest linens, china, and crystal, and provide your guests with a special culinary memory. In these days of simpler tastes and lighter appetites, the food does not have to be heavy, rich, or elaborate. The best ingredients, simply prepared and perfectly presented, know no peer. The only requirements are the proper number of courses and a pleasing contrast of flavors and textures. One other important element in giving this kind of party both style and panache is a lot of attention to detail . . . and someone else to clean up afterward!

Francisco Goya (Spanish, 1746-1828) *General Nicolas Guye*, 1810, oil on canvas. Collection of the Virginia Museum of Fine Arts, Richmond. Gift of John Lee Pratt.

RED PEPPER SOUP

2 sweet red bell peppers
6 tablespoons butter
¼ cup flour
3 cups milk
3 cups chicken broth, divided
Salt and pepper to taste
Crème Fraîche

Preheat broiler.

Halve and core peppers. Place cut side down on broiler pan and broil about 10 minutes until skin is black and blistered. Remove and place in paper bag. Close and let steam 10 minutes. Slip skins off and cut pepper into pieces. Set aside.

Melt butter and stir in flour. Add milk and simmer until thickened.

Place 2 cups chicken broth in blender. Add red pepper pieces and blend, leaving a few flecks of pepper for color and texture.

Pour pepper mixture into milk mixture and add remaining broth. Stir together. Add salt and pepper to taste. Heat through.

Garnish with dollop of Crème Fraîche.

Serves 6

CRÈME FRAÎCHE

½ cup low-fat plain yogurt
½ cup sour cream
½ cup heavy cream

Gently stir together yogurt, sour cream, and heavy cream until blended.

Store in airtight jar in refrigerator. Stir before using. May be used immediately, but tastes better after 24 hours. Keeps 2 weeks.

Yields 2 cups

SCALLOPS WITH MUSHROOMS IN SHELLS

½ cup butter at room temperature, divided
1 cup thinly sliced, fresh mushrooms
3 tablespoons finely chopped shallots
1 tablespoon finely chopped garlic
1 pound fresh bay scallops
½ cup soft breadcrumbs
½ cup finely chopped, fresh parsley
Salt and pepper to taste
6 seafood baking shells

Preheat oven to 450°.

Melt ¼ cup of butter in small skillet and cook mushrooms, stirring often, until they are wilted and give up their liquid. Add shallots and garlic and cook briefly.

Spoon mushroom mixture into medium-sized bowl. Cool 2 to 3 minutes, add 2 tablespoons of remaining butter, scallops, breadcrumbs, parsley, and salt and pepper to taste. Blend well.

Divide among 6 seafood baking shells. Arrange on baking sheet, melt remaining butter, and pour over mixture in shells. Bake 10 minutes, then place under broiler until nicely brown on top, about 1 minute.

Serves 6

THREE-FRUIT SORBET

2 cups sugar
3 cups water
5 oranges
5 lemons
I banana
3 egg whites

Boil sugar and water 5 minutes. Cool. Grate rinds of 2 oranges and 2 lemons. Add to syrup. Juice all the oranges and lemons, strain, and add to syrup.

Purée banana in blender and add to syrup. Beat egg whites stiff and fold into syrup. Pour into bowl or pan and freeze. When slushy, stir well and return to freezer. Stir several times more before serving.

Serves 6 to 8

SWEDISH VEAL ROLLETTES

8 ⅛-inch-thick slices ham
8 ⅛-inch-thick slices veal
4 tablespoons margarine or butter
½ cup dry white wine
8 ounces Swiss cheese, shredded

Place I slice ham on I slice veal, roll up, and secure with toothpick. Repeat for remainder of ham and veal.

Melt margarine in heavy skillet over medium heat and brown rollettes on all sides. Add white wine, cover, and cook over low heat until meat is tender, about 10 to 12 minutes. Remove rollettes and keep warm.

Add cheese to skillet, cook slowly, stirring constantly until cheese is melted. Spoon over rollettes.

Serves 8

PARSNIPS AND CELERY

I pound parsnips, peeled
I large bunch celery, cleaned
¼ cup coarsely chopped pecans
I tablespoon salad oil
5 tablespoons butter or margarine, divided
½ teaspoon salt

Cut parsnips and celery into 3-inch-long, matchstick strips.

In 12-inch skillet over medium heat, toast pecans until lightly browned. Remove from heat. Wipe skillet clean. Melt oil and 2 tablespoons butter over medium heat.

Add vegetables and salt, and cook about 25 to 30 minutes, or until vegetables are tender, stirring frequently. Remove to warm platter. In same skillet, melt remaining butter. Cook until butter turns golden brown, stirring constantly. Add pecans and toss to coat. Spoon over vegetables.

Serves 8 to 10

CLUB FRENCH DRESSING

4 teaspoons instant beef bouillon
3 tablespoons boiling water
I tablespoon Worcestershire sauce
I tablespoon paprika
I ½ teaspoons salt
I ½ teaspoons dry mustard
I ½ teaspoons sugar
¼ teaspoon pepper
½ cup vinegar
I cup olive or vegetable oil
4 ounces blue cheese, crumbled (optional)

✿ Dissolve bouillon in boiling water. Add Worcestershire sauce, paprika, salt, mustard, sugar, and pepper, and shake in pint jar to blend. Add vinegar and oil and shake well. Add blue cheese if desired. Store in refrigerator.

✿ Makes I ⅔ cups

CASSIS ICE CREAM

2 cups black currant preserves
I cup crème de cassis, divided
Juice of I lemon
½ teaspoon vanilla
2 cups light cream
2 cups heavy cream
⅛ teaspoon salt
Chocolate Dessert Cups
Candied Violets

✿ Mix currant preserves in blender with ½ cup cassis. Add lemon juice, remaining cassis, and vanilla.

✿ Mix together light and heavy creams with salt. Stir into currant mixture. Pour into 2 freezer trays and freeze.

✿ Serve in Chocolate Dessert Cups with a dollop of whipped cream topped with a Candied Violet.

✿ Serves 8 to I0

CHOCOLATE DESSERT CUPS AND CANDIED VIOLETS

I cup semisweet chocolate chips, melted
6 to 8 2 ½-inch paper baking cups

Candied Violets
8 perfect violets
I egg white
Sugar

✿ Place baking cups in muffin pan.

✿ Spread I heaping tablespoon melted chocolate over bottom and sides of each paper cup, covering completely. Use more chocolate if needed.

✿ Chill in refrigerator.

✿ When ready to use, peel paper away and fill cups with ice cream.

✿ Makes 6 to 8

✿ To make Candied Violets, rinse and pat violets dry.

✿ Using tiny artist's brush, brush top and bottom of each petal with egg white. Sprinkle with sugar evenly.

✿ Place on wire rack to dry.

✿ Makes 8

MOTHER'S DAY

*E*ach year on the second Sunday of May, America honors its mothers. Mother's Day was set aside as a national observance by an act of Congress in 1914, and we have celebrated it ever since.

Perhaps we as a people are of a more sentimental persuasion than most, but there is something quite touching about giving a day back to our mothers, who nurtured us, loved us, taught us, supported us, and most importantly, gave us life. Although the relationship between mother and child is constantly changing, there is usually one constant: when we need help, advice, solace, support, understanding, or someone with whom to share our joy, we usually run to Mom.

Mrs. Newton with a Child by a Pool by James Tissot presents an enchanting mother-child vignette. While Tissot cannot technically be termed an Impressionist, he comes closest to that appellation in this painting, with its outdoorsy charm and strong, loose brushwork. It is a sketch for a larger work and part of a group of paintings Tissot painted in St. John's Wood, an area of London where he lived and worked. Kathleen Kelly Newton, the artist's most frequent model, is the subject.

Mrs. Newton could be the inspiration for a Mother's Day picnic, with the family preparing and packing Mother's favorite foods and taking her to a quiet spot to enjoy a fine spring day. Or you might pamper her with a lavish

James Tissot (French, 1836-1902), *Mrs. Newton with a Child by a Pool*, ca. 1877-78, oil on mahogany panel. Collection of the Virginia Museum of Fine Arts, Richmond. Collection of Mr. and Mrs. Paul Mellon.

breakfast in bed (remember to do the dishes afterward!). Even little children can help with this one, buttering the toast, warming the croissants, arranging some daisies or roses in a vase. The family can enjoy breakfast together at a table specially set up for the occasion, keeping her company while she enjoys all this luxury and opens her presents. Among the gifts could be a promise to prepare dinner or weed the garden once a month.

Our Mother's Day celebration is a dinner served on heirloom china and linens her mother or grandmother might have used. The table

VIRGINIA PEANUT SOUP

is done in palest pink and white, with a cherubic bowl of roses, gifts adorned with tiny angels, and more miniature roses scattered about the table in silver baby cups, a nostalgic symbol of the day. Our menus reflect the bounty of spring: rack of lamb, new vegetables, fresh crab, and light-as-a-breeze desserts.

But no matter what the offering — burnt toast and jam from a five-year-old or champagne and caviar from Father — the effort will be equally appreciated. Because Mother's Day isn't about perfection, it's about caring.

Mary Cassatt (American, 1844–1926), *Baby Reaching for an Apple*, 1893. Oil on canvas. Collection of the Virginia Museum of Fine Arts, Richmond, anonymous gift, 1975.

4 tablespoons butter
1 very small onion, finely chopped
2 stalks celery, finely chopped
4 tablespoons flour
4 cups chicken broth
1 cup peanut butter
½ teaspoon salt
¼ teaspoon celery salt
2 teaspoons lemon juice
Chopped salted peanuts for garnish

Melt butter in large saucepan. Add onion and celery. Sauté 5 minutes but do not brown. Add flour and stir until well blended. Pour in chicken broth and simmer 30 minutes. Remove from heat and strain.

Stir in peanut butter, salt, celery salt, and lemon juice. Reheat but do not boil. Garnish with chopped peanuts.

Serves 6

RACK OF LAMB

2 8-rib racks of lamb
¼ cup butter
I clove garlic, pressed
½ teaspoon salt
¼ teaspoon pepper
¼ teaspoon dried whole thyme
¼ teaspoon crumbled dried rosemary
¼ cup finely minced celery

❀ Preheat oven to 375°.

❀ Trim fat to ¼ inch.

❀ Mix butter, garlic, salt, pepper, thyme, rosemary, and celery. Pat on prepared racks of lamb.

❀ Place lamb in shallow roasting pan and bake uncovered until meat thermometer registers 140° for rare or 160° for medium.

❀ Serves 4 to 6

MINT CHUTNEY
Good with lamb or pork

2 ½ cups sugar
2 ¼ teaspoons dry mustard
I ½ cups vinegar
4 cups packed fresh mint leaves
3 cups peeled, chopped tart apples
2 cups finely chopped onions
½ cup golden raisins
I teaspoon salt
4 half-pint jars

❀ In large open kettle, dissolve sugar and mustard in vinegar over low heat. Add mint, apples, onions, raisins, and salt, and bring to a boil. Reduce heat and simmer, uncovered, stirring often, about 30 minutes, or until most of liquid has evaporated.

❀ Wash and sterilize jars and tops. Pour hot chutney into hot jars and seal. Let stand one month before using.

❀ Makes 2 pints

BROCCOLI WITH ORANGE SAUCE

I pound fresh broccoli
¼ cup water
I navel orange, peeled and sectioned

Orange Sauce:
⅓ cup orange juice
½ tablespoon sugar
½ tablespoon cornstarch
Dash ginger

❀ Cut broccoli florets off stems. Put in microwave casserole, add water, cover, and microwave on high for 3 minutes. Add orange sections to broccoli and microwave for an additional 2 to 2 ½ minutes. Let stand, covered, until serving time.

❀ To make sauce, measure orange juice into glass measuring cup. Add sugar, cornstarch, and ginger. Microwave this mixture on High until thickened, about I ½ minutes. Pour over broccoli and orange sections and serve.

❀ Serves 4 to 6

MEMBERS' SUITE DRESSING
A favorite at the Virginia Museum

1 cup oil
¼ cup white wine vinegar
2 cloves garlic, minced
2 tablespoons honey
1 teaspoon dried tarragon
½ teaspoon salt
1 egg yolk
Dash Worcestershire sauce
Dash Tabasco sauce

✽ Combine all ingredients in blender or food processor fitted with steel blade. Blend until thick.

✽ Makes enough for 8 salad servings

SPOON BREAD

½ cup cornmeal
2 cups milk, divided
2 eggs
2 tablespoons butter
1 teaspoon salt
1 tablespoon sugar

✽ Preheat oven to 400°.

✽ Put cornmeal and 1 cup milk in saucepan, stir constantly and bring to a boil. Beat eggs and 1 cup milk together.

✽ Melt butter in casserole. Mix cornmeal mixture, egg mixture, salt, and sugar, and pour into casserole. Bake about 45 minutes or until brown and set.

✽ Serves 6

RASPBERRIES ON A CLOUD

Meringues:
  4 egg whites, room temperature
  ½ teaspoon cream of tartar
  1 teaspoon vanilla
  1 cup sugar
  1 cup chopped pecans (optional)

Raspberry Sauce:
  2 tablespoons cornstarch
  ⅔ cup sugar
  2 pints fresh or 2 10-ounce packages
     frozen raspberries
  2 tablespoons freshly squeezed lemon juice
  Vanilla ice cream

✽ Preheat oven to 250°.

✽ To make meringues, beat egg whites with electric mixer until frothy. Add cream of tartar and vanilla and continue beating until double in volume. Mix in sugar 1 tablespoon at a time until meringue is stiff and glossy. Fold in pecans.

✽ To form individual meringues, drop 2 tablespoons of meringue mixture onto cookie sheet lined with brown paper. Hollow out center with back of spoon to form nest. A pastry bag can also be used to flute the meringues.

☙ Bake 50 minutes. Turn off oven and leave in another 10 minutes to dry out. Store in air-tight container. Meringues freeze well.

☙ To make sauce, mix cornstarch with ⅔ cup sugar in top of double boiler over simmering water. Add raspberries and stir until thick and shiny. Add lemon juice. Refrigerate if not serving immediately.

☙ Serve meringue nest with scoop of vanilla ice cream topped with raspberry sauce.

☙ Serves 8 to 10

CRAB CASSEROLE

1 cup melted butter
3 cups milk
½ teaspoon pepper
6 eggs
1 cup biscuit mix
2 cups grated mild domestic Swiss cheese
2 pounds lump crabmeat
1 cup mayonnaise

☙ Preheat oven to 350°.

☙ Mix butter, milk, pepper, eggs, and biscuit mix in blender until smooth. Pour into 9 x 13-inch buttered glass casserole. Sprinkle with Swiss cheese.

☙ Mix crabmeat with mayonnaise and spread on top of cheese, gently pressing it down into liquid base.

☙ Bake 55 minutes. Remove from oven and let sit 10 minutes until firm.

☙ Serves 10 to 12

STUFFED BAKED TOMATOES

10 medium tomatoes
Salt and pepper
1 pound bacon, crisp cooked, drained, and crumbled
2 large onions, chopped
½ stick butter
12 to 14 slices fresh bread, cubed
1 cup sharp cheese
¼ cup water

☙ Preheat oven to 325°.

☙ Wash tomatoes. Remove and discard inside pulp. Season with salt and pepper.

☙ Sauté onions in bacon drippings. Remove to bowl with slotted spoon.

☙ In clean pan, melt butter and toss bread cubes until lightly browned.

☙ Combine bacon, onions, and bread cubes, and stuff tomatoes firmly. Top with cheese and place in casserole dish. Add water. Bake 20 minutes.

☙ Serves 10

GRAPEFRUIT AND AVOCADO SALAD WITH SHALLOT SALAD DRESSING

I grapefruit, peeled and sectioned
I avocado, peeled and cut into ½" slices
I shallot, chopped
Juice of I lemon or 2 tablespoons
2 tablespoons sugar
I tablespoon Dijon mustard
I teaspoon celery salt
¼ cup balsamic vinegar
I cup olive oil and vegetable oil, combined

❈ Combine all ingredients, except grapefruit and avocado, in blender and mix well.

❈ Pour over grapefruit and avocado.

❈ Makes about I ½ cups

POPOVERS

I cup whole or skim milk
I cup flour
3 eggs
4 tablespoons melted butter or margarine
I teaspoon salt

❈ Preheat oven to 425°.

❈ Mix all ingredients and put in greased muffin tin. Bake 30 minutes.

❈ Makes I dozen

ALMOND RUM CREAM PIE

⅔ cup superfine granulated sugar
⅓ cup cake flour
Generous dash salt
2 large eggs, slightly beaten
8 tablespoons rum, divided
I ½ cups milk, scalded
9-inch crumb pie shell, chilled
½ cup almonds, blanched and toasted
I cup heavy cream, whipped
½ cup shaved unsweetened chocolate
9-inch crumb pie shell, chilled

❈ Stir sugar, flour, and salt in top of double boiler. Add eggs and 3 tablespoons rum, and blend well.

❈ Stir 5 tablespoons rum very gradually (drop by drop to prevent curdling) into scalded milk. Add milk mixture to sugar and egg mixture and cook over hot water, stirring constantly, until thickened. Cool.

❈ Sprinkle crumb crust with almonds. Pour rum cream mixture over almonds. Cover with whipped cream and shaved chocolate. Chill.

❈ Serves 6 to 8

Early Suppers

PONY ROUNDUP

CHINCOTEAGUE

*C*hincoteague is Virginia's only resort island. As the gateway to the National Seashore and Chincoteague Wildlife Refuge, this pleasant fishing village is rich in both history and natural charm. Although a book and a movie have made its "wild" ponies famous, its recreational diversity and its small-town courtesy also lure visitors from all over the world. Those who enjoy the sea, boating, fishing, and crabbing will find Chincoteague irresistible.

Chincoteague's famous salt oysters, with their distinctive piquant flavor, have been sold commercially since 1830. They are cultivated on leased rock and public grounds that the watermen seed and harvest as you would your vegetable garden. Those who enjoy crabbing can catch their dinner in no time as the "crop" is so plentiful. Chincoteague is also home to many outstanding artists who produce some of the world's finest duck decoys and waterfowl reproductions. It is that rare combination, a get-away-from-it-all place with plenty to do.

The ponies, however, are the top draw. Every July as many as 45,000 people (or more) flood in for the Pony Roundup. The roundup has benefited the local fire department since 1924, when two disastrous fires nearly leveled the town because of inadequate firefighting equipment.

According to legend, some time in the 16th century a Spanish galleon with a cargo of mustangs wrecked off the Assateague coast; some of the animals swam to safety and their descendants still graze there today. These sturdy little horses played an important part in the history of the islands, as they were used for both transportation and pulling power. Now the main tourist attraction, they regularly cause "pony jams" as people stop their cars to offer them treats or pet them.

The Pony Roundup starts with corralling the ponies into pens, where they are kept to rest a day or two. Crowds gather along the shore in the morning to watch the famous swim across Assateague Channel. After another rest, the animals are paraded down Main Street, and the pony auction begins. Children, wide-eyed with desire at the thought of owning a real Chincoteague pony, watch the bidding to see if one of these winning little equines will accompany them home.

The relationship between people and horses, whether rough-coated wild ponies or Arabian stallions, has always been unique, marked with a special interdependency and respect. Among the many equine images in the Virginia Museum, *In the Marais* (next page) by John R. Skeaping best fits the mood and idea of Chincoteague. With its silvered mist, its marsh grasses, and its flying manes and hooves, this lively painting captures the almost mystical spirit of the horse.

John R. Skeaping (English, 1901-1980), *In the Marais*, 1975, watercolor and gouache. Collection of the Virginia Museum of Fine Arts, Richmond. The Paul Mellon Collection.

From the age of three, Skeaping began his love affair with horses; his childhood dream was to become a jockey. But his passion for drawing animals won out, and at age 13 he enrolled in the Blackheath School of Art in England. There he also began to master working in clay, wood, and stone, earning a place in sculpture at the Royal Academy Schools in London. In 1924, when the first pony roundup began at Chincoteague, Skeaping had just won the Prix de Rome for sculpture. He did statues of the famous racehorses in England, Ireland, and France and is regarded as the master in depicting animals in action.

The charming pottery used in our menu photograph, with a different animal on each piece, is the work of an Eastern Shore resident, artist José Dovis. These are fitting containers for our seaside dinners after the exhilaration of the day. Since Pony Roundup is in July, none of those succulent Chincoteague oysters are featured on the menu, but if you plan to prepare these menus any time from September through April, you simply must include them.

Since wonderful fresh produce is also grown in this area, we've taken advantage of the plenitude of both sea and shore. From crab cakes, clam fritters, and chowder, to piquant vegetable dishes and cooling chilled-fruit desserts, almost everything can be at least partially prepared ahead of time, so the cook can enjoy the festivities, too.

Even if you can't get to Chincoteague, these dinners are perfect summer fare and will be equally welcomed by family and guests in your own backyard. You might even invite a few nice ponies!

CHINCOTEAGUE CLAM CHOWDER

2 pounds clams, chopped, drained,
   reserving juice
2 cups diced potatoes
I cup diced celery
I cup diced onion
Water
¾ cup flour
¾ cup butter or margarine, melted
I quart whole milk
4 slices bacon
I ½ teaspoons or less salt
Pepper
Seasoned salt to taste
I ½ teaspoons thyme

In large saucepan, pour clam juice over potatoes, celery, and onions and add enough water to cover vegetables. Cover and simmer about 20 minutes.

In another saucepan, blend flour into melted butter until smooth. Gradually add milk, blending well. Cook over moderate heat, stirring constantly, until mixture is bubbly hot and thickened.

Fry bacon until crisp. Drain and crumble. Add vegetables, liquids, clams, and bacon. Add salt, pepper, seasoned salt, and thyme.

Heat thoroughly but do not boil.

Serves 8

SPICY CRAB CAKES

½ cup soft whole-wheat or white
   breadcrumbs
⅓ cup chopped onion
⅓ cup chopped celery
2 tablespoons reduced-calorie mayonnaise
2 teaspoons minced fresh basil
I teaspoon Dijon mustard
I teaspoon Worcestershire sauce
⅛ teaspoon cayenne pepper
2 eggs, well beaten
I pound fresh lump crabmeat
Vegetable-oil cooking spray

Combine breadcrumbs, onion, celery, mayonnaise, basil, mustard, Worcestershire sauce, cayenne pepper, and eggs. Mix well.

Add crabmeat gently to breadcrumb mixture, trying not to break up lumps. Divide mixture into 6 equal portions, shaping each into a ½-inch-thick patty. Cover and chill I hour.

Spray nonstick skillet with cooking spray, and cook crab cakes over medium-low heat until browned, about 5 minutes per side.

Makes 4

SCALLOPED CABBAGE

*This is a good vegetable to serve with
ham, beef, veal, or lamb.*

I medium head green cabbage, sliced
3 cloves garlic, minced
3 tablespoons butter
Salt and pepper to taste
I cup heavy cream
Paprika

Preheat oven to 325°.

Sauté cabbage and garlic in butter in covered frying pan until tender and slightly brown. Add salt and pepper, then cream. Place in buttered 2-quart casserole and bake 25 minutes. Sprinkle with paprika.

Serves 4

BLACK BEAN AND RICE SALAD

¾ cup long-grain rice, cooked
1 16-ounce can black beans, washed and
   drained
¼ teaspoon pepper
1 8-ounce bottle zesty Italian salad dressing
Mixed lettuce leaves
¾ cup shredded cheddar cheese
1 medium tomato, chopped
3 green onions, thinly sliced
Sour cream (optional)

Mix rice with beans, pepper, and salad
dressing, and allow to marinate overnight in
refrigerator.

At serving time, place on mixed lettuce
leaves and top with cheese, tomatoes, and
onions.

Put a dollop of sour cream on top, if desired.
"Boil in bag" rice can be used; Romano cheese
can be substituted for cheddar.

Serves 8

ENGLISH MUFFIN LOAF BREAD

6 cups flour, divided
2 packages active dry yeast
1 tablespoon sugar
2 teaspoons salt
¼ teaspoon baking soda
2 cups milk
½ cup water
Cornmeal

Combine 3 cups flour, yeast, sugar, salt, and
baking soda.

Heat milk and water until very warm (120°
to 130°). Add to dry ingredients and beat
well. Stir in remaining flour to make a stiff
batter.

Grease two 8 ½ x 4 ½ x 2 ½-inch loaf pans,
and sprinkle with cornmeal. Spoon batter into
pans and sprinkle tops with cornmeal. Cover
and let rise in warm place 45 minutes.

Preheat oven to 400°. Bake 25 minutes.
Remove from pans and cool on rack.

Makes 2 loaves

LEMON ZEST PIE

1 lemon, well chopped with seeds removed
4 eggs
1 stick margarine, softened
2 cups sugar
2 tablespoons milk
1 unbaked 9-inch pie shell

Preheat oven to 375°.

Blend lemon with eggs and margarine in
blender. Add sugar and milk to mixture and
blend.

Pour mixture into pie shell and bake 30
minutes.

Serves 6 to 8

CLAM FRITTERS
An Eastern Shore specialty

1 teaspoon dehydrated onions
1 egg, well beaten
1 cup drained, minced clams
¼ cup flour
½ teaspoon baking powder
⅛ teaspoon black pepper
2 tablespoons vegetable oil
2 tablespoons margarine

Stir onion and egg into clams. Combine flour, baking powder, and pepper, and add to clams.

Heat oil and margarine until hot. Drop batter by tablespoon into hot fat and cook until browned. Serve immediately.

Serves 4

VIRGINIA FRIED CORN

6 slices bacon
3 cups corn kernels, pulp, and milk, scraped off cob
1 teaspoon salt
⅛ teaspoon pepper
1 teaspoon sugar

Sauté bacon in skillet until crisp. Drain well. In same skillet, add corn to drippings and cook 5 to 10 minutes or until thickened. Stir often. Season with salt, pepper, and sugar. Crumble bacon over top.

Serves 4

Fried Okra Salad

6 slices bacon
1 10-ounce package frozen sliced okra, defrosted
2 tomatoes, chopped
1 bunch green onions, chopped with tops
½ cup chopped green pepper
Salt and pepper to taste

Dressing:
¼ cup vinegar
¼ cup sugar
½ cup oil

Sauté bacon until crisp. Drain, then crumble. Sauté okra and drain on paper towels.

Mix okra, bacon, tomatoes, onions, and green pepper together. Add salt and pepper.

Mix dressing ingredients together and pour over vegetables. Toss well.

Serves 4

Black Iron Skillet Corn Bread

2 tablespoons canola oil
1 cup buttermilk
1 egg
½ teaspoon salt
1 teaspoon sugar
1 teaspoon baking powder
½ teaspoon baking soda
1 cup stone-ground yellow cornmeal
1 8-inch, well-seasoned black iron skillet (essential)

Preheat oven to 400°. Put oil in skillet and place skillet in oven until it is very hot.

Beat buttermilk and egg until blended. Add salt, sugar, baking powder, baking soda, and cornmeal.

Carefully remove skillet from oven, pour batter into skillet, and put back in oven to bake about 20 minutes, or until brown and crunchy.

Serves 4

BLUEBERRY SURPRISE

Meringue shells:
   4 egg whites
   1 teaspoon vanilla
   ¼ teaspoon cream of tartar
   Dash salt
   1 cup sugar

Filling:
   2 pints blueberries
   ⅔ cup Frangelica liqueur
   Sugar to taste if sour

Topping:
   1 cup whipping cream
   2 tablespoons powdered sugar

Preheat oven to 275°.

To make meringue shells, making sure beaters and bowl are absolutely clean, whip egg whites until foamy. Add vanilla, cream of tartar, and salt. While continuing to beat, add sugar 1 tablespoon at a time until mixture stands in peaks.

Line cookie sheet with unglazed paper and draw 8 circles 3 or 4 inches in diameter. Fill circles with meringue mixture, making a depression in center with spoon.

Bake 1 hour. Turn off heat and leave meringues in oven one more hour or overnight.

Pull off paper and store in airtight container. Do not attempt to make these on a rainy day.

To make filling, wash, drain, and pick over berries.

Toss with Frangelica and refrigerate until serving time. Sweeten if necessary.

To make topping, whip cream and add powdered sugar.

To assemble, top each meringue with berries and a dollop of whipped cream.

May also use 1 pint raspberries mixed with ½ cup sugar and ⅓ cup Chambord liqueur; 1 pint strawberries mixed with sugar to taste and ⅓ cup Grand Marnier liqueur; or 1 pint blackberries mixed with ¾ cup sugar and ⅓ cup light rum.

Serves 8

SUPER BOWL PARTY

MENUS

Bacon Cheddar Spread *with* Crackers

Rye Nibbles

Quarterback Chili *served with* Corn Chips,
Chopped Green Onions, *and* Grated Cheese

Cole Slaw

Lahvash (Cracker Bread)

Fluffy Frosty Peanut Pie Tarts

Layered Seafood Tray

Beer Nuts

Cassoulet

Autumn Tossed Salad

Hard Rolls

Second-Half Goody Tray *of* Mock Toffee,
Chess Bars, *and* Cappuccino Squares

Bowl *of* Apples *and* Pears

---

*E*ver since that fateful Sunday in 1967, when the Green Bay Packers clashed with the Kansas City Chiefs in Los Angeles (and, for all you football trivia buffs, Green Bay won, 35 to 10), the Super Bowl has become an American institution, second only to the Fourth of July and Thanksgiving. Neither snow, nor sleet, nor rain, nor even an occasional war interferes with the playing out of this drama! Ask most American males their favorite way to entertain, and odds are the answer will be "Super Bowl Party!"

The reasons are obvious — informality, the camaraderie of friends, good-natured rivalry, hearty food. One doesn't have to think of dressing up, of engaging in polite conversation, of pouring the right wine. One certainly doesn't think of how many calories are being ingested.

Even long-suffering women (who virtually say good-bye to the men in their lives at the onset of football season) like it. The food usually requires only one utensil (most often a fork), is eaten out of hand or on a tray, and can be prepared up to two days in advance. The remnants, if there are any, are a quick cleanup. All of this ensures that at least half the guests will go home happy — the losers will have to wait until next year.

We include two menus for early Super Bowl suppers, intended to be served during halftime. Your recipe files will undoubtedly yield many more. Main dishes and desserts can be made up to two days ahead, salads and snacks the morning of the game or one day before. All the dishes are essentially "male" food: robust, filling, and hearty. (This is no time for Nouvelle!) Desserts are finger foods to be nibbled during the second half: cookies, tarts, bars, and fruits.

The personification of the Super Bowl, the ultimate contact game, is Wayne Thiebaud's *Football Player* (next page) from the Virginia Museum collection. Thiebaud first gained national recognition with his still life of heavily painted rows of cakes, pies, and candies, represented as icons of a consumer society. Because of his focus on "countertop culture," Thiebaud was alternately called the "Pie Man" and the "Poet-Laureate of the Coffee Break." He described himself as a "sign painter gone uppity."

In 1963, the year Thiebaud painted his *Football Player,* the artist decided to try a different subject, the human figure. His technique remained the same as the one he had used for his paintings of foods, with the subject emphasized against a white background and outlined in thick multicolored bands, as if it had been painted and is being viewed under strong artificial light. The figure is factual and recognizable, but enigmatic and somehow larger than life — which is just the way we like our football heroes to be.

Wayne Thiebaud (American, born 1920), *Football Player*, 1963, oil on canvas. Collection of the Virginia Museum of Fine Arts, Richmond. Gift of The Sydney and Frances Lewis Foundation.

BACON CHEDDAR SPREAD

1 cup extra-sharp cheddar cheese
1 ½ tablespoons finely chopped onion
½ cup mayonnaise
¼ cup chopped pecans
2 slices bacon, crisp cooked and crumbled

Blend all ingredients and store in tightly covered container in refrigerator.

Makes a great sandwich, cracker spread, or cheese ball.

Serves 8

RYE NIBBLES

26 slices party rye bread
1 stick butter or margarine, melted
Garlic salt
Parmesan cheese

Preheat oven to 200°.

Cut bread into thirds and place on cookie sheet. Brush or drizzle with melted butter. Lightly sprinkle with garlic salt.

Place in oven 45 minutes. Turn and repeat butter and garlic salt. Return to oven 30 minutes.

Sprinkle with Parmesan cheese and return to oven 5 minutes.

Store in airtight container.

Can also be made with pita bread or other favorite.

Makes 78

QUARTERBACK CHILI

1 tablespoon vegetable oil
1 clove garlic, minced
1 jalapeño pepper, minced
1 cup chopped onion
1 cup chopped green pepper
2 pounds coarsely ground beef
1 ½ tablespoons chili powder
1 tablespoon cumin
1 tablespoon paprika
1 ½ teaspoons salt
½ teaspoon black pepper
¼ teaspoon cayenne pepper
1 6-ounce can tomato paste
1 ½ cups water
2 16-ounce cans pinto beans,
    drained and rinsed

Pour oil in large, heavy pot and sauté garlic, jalapeño pepper, onion, and green pepper until limp. Add beef and cook slowly until meat is slightly brown. Add chili powder, cumin, paprika, salt, and black and cayenne peppers. Mix well. Add tomato paste and water. Stir until blended. Cook on very low heat 15 minutes.

When ready to serve, add beans and heat thoroughly.

Serve with chopped green onions, grated cheese, and corn chips on the side.

Serves 8

COLE SLAW
This tangy slaw keeps well for days.

I cup finely chopped onion
I cup finely chopped green pepper
I large head cabbage, shredded
I cup sugar
I cup vinegar
¾ cup vegetable oil
I teaspoon dry mustard
I teaspoon celery seed
I teaspoon salt or to taste

Combine onion, green pepper, and cabbage in large bowl.

Combine sugar, vinegar, vegetable oil, mustard, celery seed, and salt. Bring to a boil. Pour hot dressing mixture over cabbage mixture, cover well, and refrigerate at least 4 hours to let flavors blend.

Serves 8 to 10

FLUFFY FROSTY PEANUT PIE TARTS

4 ounces cream cheese, softened
I cup powdered sugar
½ cup creamy peanut butter
½ cup milk
9 ounces whipped topping
8 cookie-crumb tart shells
¼ cup finely chopped salted peanuts
Whipped topping for garnish if desired

In large bowl, whip cream cheese until soft and fluffy. Beat in sugar and peanut butter. Add milk slowly, blending thoroughly. Fold in whipped topping.

Pour into individual tart shells. Sprinkle with chopped peanuts. Freeze until firm; allow to stand at room temperature 10 minutes before serving.

If desired, garnish with more whipped topping. This filling can also be used in a 9-inch graham cracker pie crust or chocolate crumb crust.

Makes 8 tarts or I pie

LAYERED SEAFOOD TRAY

8 ounces cream cheese, softened
½ cup sour cream
¼ teaspoon onion salt
Dash red pepper
Dash lemon pepper
¼ cup plus I tablespoon chili sauce
I ½ teaspoons Worcestershire sauce
¾ teaspoon lemon juice
½ teaspoon horseradish
¼ teaspoon whole tarragon
½ pound crabmeat or ½ pound shrimp, cooked and cleaned

Combine softened cream cheese, sour cream, onion salt, and peppers. Shape into 5-inch circle, 1-inch thick, on serving platter. Cover and refrigerate at least 30 minutes.

Combine chili sauce, Worcestershire sauce, lemon juice, horseradish, and tarragon, and spread over chilled cream cheese mixture. Top with crabmeat or shrimp or ½-pound combination of both.

Serve with assorted crackers. May be prepared I day in advance except for adding seafood.

Serves 8 to 10

CASSOULET

1 pound dried navy beans
1 cup chopped onion
2 whole cloves
1 bay leaf
1 sprig parsley
1 teaspoon salt
3 tablespoons butter, divided
1 pound fresh pork sausage
1 onion, sliced
1 clove garlic, minced
1 pound ground beef
Salt and pepper to taste
1 pound smoked Polish sausage
1 cup dry white wine
1 8-ounce can tomato sauce
½ teaspoon thyme

Preheat oven to 350°.

Soak beans overnight as directed on package. Drain.

Cook beans in 2 quarts fresh water with onion, cloves, bay leaf, parsley, and 1 teaspoon salt until tender. Set aside, reserving liquid.

Heat 1 tablespoon butter in skillet, add pork sausage and cook until crumbly but not dry. Add onion and garlic, and cook until soft. Drain excess fat.

Crumble beef in separate skillet and cook until no longer pink. Add salt and pepper to taste. Brown Polish sausage in skillet with beef and cut into ¼-inch slices.

Drain beans, reserving liquid.

In 3-quart casserole, layer ½ beans and ½ meat mixture. Repeat layers.

Add wine, tomato sauce, 1 cup of bean liquid, and thyme to skillet. Heat and simmer a few minutes, then pour over cassoulet.

Bake 1 hour. If cassoulet becomes dry, add reserved liquid.

Serves 8

AUTUMN TOSSED SALAD

½ cup Italian salad dressing, divided
2 ounces blue cheese, divided
3 unpeeled, cored, tart red apples
1 head lettuce or 8 cups broken-up
   lettuce leaves
1 small red onion, peeled

In large salad bowl pour ¼ cup salad dressing and add 1 ounce blue cheese. Mash cheese into dressing and blend until smooth.

Slice apples into thin wedges and toss in salad dressing mixture to coat well. Refrigerate.

At serving time, add lettuce, thinly sliced red onion, and remaining blue cheese, crumbled.

Toss well with remaining salad dressing.

Serves 8

MOCK TOFFEE

1 sleeve saltine crackers
1 cup sugar
2 sticks butter or 1 stick butter and
    1 stick margarine
12 ounces chocolate chips
1 cup chopped pecans

❧ Preheat oven to 325°.

❧ Cover jelly-roll pan with foil. Cover foil with crackers placed close together.

❧ Mix sugar and butter, cook 3 minutes, and pour over crackers. Bake 15 minutes.

❧ While hot, cover with chocolate chips and spread with knife.

❧ Sprinkle with pecans.

❧ Cool and break into pieces.

❧ Serves 12

CHESS BARS

½ cup butter
1 cup plus 2 tablespoons all-purpose flour,
    divided
1 ½ cups light brown sugar, divided
2 eggs, beaten
¼ teaspoon baking powder
¼ teaspoon salt
1 teaspoon vanilla
1 cup chopped pecans
1 3 ½-ounce can flaked coconut
1 ½ cups powdered sugar
2 tablespoons orange juice
2 tablespoons lemon juice
Grated rind of 1 lemon

❧ Preheat oven to 350°.

❧ To make crust, blend butter, 1 cup flour, and ½ cup brown sugar, and pat in bottom of greased 8 x 12-inch pan. Bake 10 minutes or until lightly browned.

❧ To make filling, combine eggs, 1 cup brown sugar, 2 tablespoons flour, baking powder, salt, and vanilla. Fold in pecans and coconut. Pour on top of crust and return to oven for about 30 minutes.

❧ To make glaze, combine powdered sugar, orange juice, lemon juice, and lemon rind. Spread glaze over filling while warm. Cool and cut into bars.

❧ Makes 27

CAPPUCCINO SQUARES

2 sticks butter or margarine
1 8-ounce package unsweetened chocolate
3 ½ cups sugar
6 large eggs
1 8-ounce can (2 cups) walnuts,
    coarsely chopped
1 ¾ cups all-purpose flour
¼ cup instant espresso coffee powder
2 teaspoons vanilla
½ teaspoon cinnamon
½ teaspoon salt
Powdered sugar for garnish

❧ Preheat oven to 350°. Grease and flour 9 x 13-inch baking pan.

❧ In heavy saucepan over low heat, melt butter and chocolate, stirring often. Remove from heat and whisk in sugar and eggs until well blended. Stir in walnuts, flour, espresso powder, vanilla, cinnamon, and salt.

❧ Spread evenly in pan and bake 45 to 50 minutes or until tested done. Cool completely in pan on wire rack. Cut crosswise into 6 strips, then cut each strip into 4 pieces. Sprinkle top half of each square with powdered sugar.

❧ Store in single layer in tightly covered container. May be made 1 day ahead.

❧ Makes 2 dozen

Late Suppers

AFTER THE BALLET
RICHMOND

MENUS

Hot Seafood Salad

Smoked Ham *with* Apricot Honey Glaze

Mustard Mousse

Broccoli *with* Red Onion Vinaigrette

Fresh Fruit Tray *with* Coconut Bananas

Sherry Pound Cake *with* Fabulous Fudge
Sauce *and* Whole Fresh Strawberries

Cold Poached Salmon *with* Dill Sauce

Thinly Sliced Beef Tenderloin
with Fluffy Horseradish Cream

Bulgur Pilaf

Tomato Scallop

Zesty Green Beans

Sherwood Forest Orange Cream Sauce

Frances's Angel Food Cake

Who among us has never danced? Music and dance, the languages of the heart, seem to rely more on human instinct than on invention for their expression. Even young babies will respond to rhythm. By our very nature, we do not have to be taught to "jump for joy."

Perhaps no form of dance has crossed more national and cultural boundaries than ballet, and none has remained both so classic and yet so in touch with the changing times. Derived from the Italian word *ballare*, to dance, it was originally a court spectacle for which both audience and performers were drawn exclusively from the nobility. Ballet became popular as early as the 18th century, when itinerant dancing troupes gave performances all over Europe and even in America. Its popularization continued sporadically, and was aided greatly at the beginning of this century by Anna Pavlova's tireless world tours. It was she who brought ballet to thousands who had never suspected its existence.

Ballet was probably introduced to the American colonies by Henry Holt, a London dancer who presented *Harlequin and Scaramouche* in Charleston, South Carolina, in 1735. But it was not until the French Revolution uprooted great numbers of artists that performances here became frequent events. Romantic ballet reached its peak in America with the visit of the great Austrian ballerina Fanny Elssler in 1840. When she danced in Washington, D.C., Congress was obliged to recess because it could not obtain a quorum.

Virginians have traditionally loved and supported ballet, and the Richmond Ballet, the city's own resident company, has grown from a small civic endeavor in 1958 to a professional company of 17 dancers in a corps that also includes apprentices and selected students. The 14-year-old School of the Richmond Ballet merged with the Ballet Company in 1985, and in 1990 the Richmond Ballet was proclaimed the State Ballet of Virginia by Governor L. Douglas Wilder. Each season's ambitious schedule offers classic and contemporary ballet and premieres new works. The Richmond Ballet today plays to its broadest audience ever, so that its viewers in Richmond, across Virginia, and throughout the Southeast can see dance in its most encompassing form and at its very best.

Few works of art personify ballet better than Edgar Degas' *Little Dancer, Fourteen Years Old* (next page). Although Degas was known primarily for his oils and pastels, he also worked in sculpture. None of his wax and clay models were cast before his death, and only one of his wax sculptures, the *Little Dancer*, was exhibited publicly during his lifetime. Of the 20 figures cast after Degas' death, the Virginia Museum's *Dancer* is one of the two set aside for the artist's own heirs.

The rough, sketchy texture of the original

wax model, and hence of the cast bronze, enlivens the surface with dappled light. The young dancer is caught between movements — one has just been completed, another is about to follow. The bronze casts in this series all wear actual gauze skirts and satin hair ribbons, a touch of realism that adds magic to this charming piece.

After an evening at the ballet, you'll want the elegant mood to last, so we've set a sophisticated late supper in a penthouse with the starry skyline of Richmond twinkling below. Here the difference is drama and understatement, with perfect single blossoms nodding in tall stems of crystal (much like the *corps de ballet* itself) reflecting an abundance of candlelight. You could set your table with whatever props you may have on hand: a pair of ballet slippers, a nosegay of roses surrounded by a frill of tutu-like tulle, programs from past performances, porcelain swans with stargazer lilies or a parade of nutcrackers, especially if you've just seen *Swan Lake* or *The Nutcracker*.

The menu we've chosen can be largely prepared in advance to be easily assembled and presented while everyone enjoys a celebratory glass of champagne. The hot seafood salad and glazed smoked ham with zesty mustard mousse provide warming flavor contrasts on a frosty night, while the cold salmon and tenderloin followed by a meltingly light and creamy angel food dessert are perfect early spring or autumn fare.

After an evening like this, with the wonderful melding of dance, music, food, wine, and atmosphere, you really know what harmony is!

Edgar Degas (French, 1834-1917), *Little Dancer, Fourteen Years Old (Petite Danseuse de quatorze ans)*, bronze, net, satin. Collection of the Virginia Museum of Fine Arts, Richmond. Purchase, State Operating Funds and The Art Lovers' Society Fund.

HOT SEAFOOD SALAD

¼ cup minced onion
3 tablespoons butter, divided
¾ pound shrimp, cooked, shelled, and deveined
I cup (½ pound) backfin crabmeat
½ cup chopped green pepper
I cup sliced celery
I cup mayonnaise
I teaspoon Worcestershire sauce
½ teaspoon salt
¼ teaspoon pepper
½ cup fresh breadcrumbs

❧ Preheat oven to 350°.

❧ Sauté onion in 2 tablespoons butter. Combine onion, shrimp, crabmeat, green peppers, celery, mayonnaise, Worcestershire sauce, salt, and pepper. Pour into 2 ½-quart casserole.

❧ Top with breadcrumbs and remaining one tablespoon melted butter.

❧ Bake 30 minutes.

❧ Serves 6

SMOKED HAM WITH APRICOT HONEY GLAZE

1 smoked ham, fully cooked
½ cup apricot jam
½ cup honey
1 tablespoon cornstarch
4 tablespoons lemon juice
½ teaspoon ground cloves
1 teaspoon dried mustard
Whole cloves

Preheat oven to 325°.

Wipe ham with wet cloth. Put fat side up in pan. Cover bottom of pan with small amount of water. Do not cover. Bake approximately 15 minutes per pound. To decorate, remove ham from oven 30 minutes before done. Remove rind and excess fat. Score remaining fat with diamond design.

To make glaze, combine jam, honey, cornstarch, lemon juice, ground cloves, and mustard in saucepan. Heat, stirring constantly, until thickened and bubbly, at least 10 minutes. Spread glaze over ham, put one clove in center of each diamond and cook 30 minutes more. Cool before carving.

MUSTARD MOUSSE

1 tablespoon unflavored gelatin
2 tablespoons cold water
2 tablespoons dry white wine
¾ cup sour cream
1 cup mayonnaise
1 tablespoon horseradish
¼ cup chopped chives
¼ cup brown mustard
1 tablespoon dry mustard
1 teaspoon lemon juice
Few drops Tabasco sauce

Soak gelatin in cold water. Heat mixture until gelatin is dissolved. Add wine. Mix sour cream, mayonnaise, horseradish, chives, mustards, lemon juice, and Tabasco sauce. Add to gelatin mixture. Pour into 1 ½-pint mold and refrigerate until set. Serve with ham.

Makes 1 ½ pints

BROCCOLI WITH RED ONION VINAIGRETTE

1 bunch (about 1 ½ to 2 pounds) broccoli
3 tablespoons vegetable oil
1 tablespoon red wine vinegar
½ teaspoon Dijon mustard
⅛ teaspoon salt
⅛ teaspoon pepper
½ cup thinly sliced purple onion rings

Steam broccoli until tender crisp. Drain and keep steamer covered. To make vinaigrette, combine oil, vinegar, mustard, salt, and pepper. Add onion rings and vinaigrette to broccoli, and let stand 5 minutes. Onion will be slightly cooked.

Serves 4 to 6

COCONUT BANANAS

3 tablespoons lemon juice
½ pint sour cream
⅛ teaspoon salt
4 cups shredded coconut
4 bananas, peeled

❧ Place lemon juice, sour cream with salt, and coconut in 3 separate bowls.

❧ Slice 1 banana at a time into ½-inch pieces, dip slices into lemon juice, turn in sour cream, and roll in coconut, covering all sides.

❧ Place on tray, 1 layer deep. Cover with plastic wrap and refrigerate several hours or overnight.

❧ Serves 8 to 10

SHERRY POUND CAKE
Its flavor is even better after freezing.

2 sticks butter
3 cups sugar
3 cups all-purpose flour
½ pint sour cream
¼ teaspoon baking soda
6 eggs
1 teaspoon vanilla
4 to 6 tablespoons sherry

❧ Preheat oven to 300°.

❧ Cream butter and sugar. Add flour and sour cream mixed with baking soda, alternately.

❧ Add eggs, one at a time, beating well after each addition. Add vanilla and sherry.

❧ Grease and flour 10-inch tube pan and pour in batter. Bake 1 ½ hours.

❧ Makes about 24 thin slices

FABULOUS FUDGE SAUCE

4 ounces unsweetened chocolate
2 tablespoons butter or margarine
2 cups sugar
½ teaspoon salt
1 cup whole milk
1 can sweetened condensed milk
1 teaspoon vanilla

❧ In double boiler, melt chocolate and butter. Add sugar, salt, whole milk, and condensed milk. Cook 20 minutes, stirring often. Beat with spoon. Add vanilla. Cook an additional 5 to 10 minutes.

❧ Pour into 2 wide-mouthed pint jars. Chill.

❧ This may be frozen. To serve, thaw overnight. Remove top and heat in jar in pan of water.

❧ Makes 4 cups

COLD POACHED SALMON WITH DILL SAUCE

Bouquet garni:
 1 bay leaf
 1 sprig parsley
 1 sprig thyme
 Top of 1 stalk celery

 1 6-pound salmon, gutted, with head
  and tail still on
 1 750-milliliter bottle dry white wine
 2 quarts water
 1 carrot, peeled and sliced
 1 onion, sliced
 1 tablespoon salt
 6 peppercorns

Dill sauce:
 1 cup reduced-calorie mayonnaise
 1 cup plain low-fat yogurt
 1 tablespoon Dijon mustard
 ½ cup minced fresh dill
 Salt and pepper

To make bouquet garni, place bay leaf, parsley, thyme, and celery in small square of cheesecloth. Pull up corners and tie securely.

Wrap fish in double thickness of cheesecloth. Bring wine and water to a boil in fish poacher. Add bouquet garni, carrot, onion, salt, and peppercorns. Lower salmon into liquid. Gently simmer about 1 hour or until fish flakes when tested with a fork.

Remove fish from liquid, unwrap, and remove skin.

To make dill sauce, combine and blend all ingredients. Chill.

Serve fish with dill sauce and garnish as desired.

Serves 8 to 10

BEEF TENDERLOIN

 1 5- to 7-pound tenderloin, at room
  temperature
 Salt and pepper to taste

Preheat oven to 400°.

Place meat on broiler rack and place in oven. Immediately reduce heat to 325° and cook 40 to 45 minutes.

Remove from oven. Sprinkle with salt and pepper and let stand at least 15 minutes before slicing. Meat will be medium rare.

Serves 10 to 12

FLUFFY HORSERADISH CREAM

I cup whipping cream
3 tablespoons sugar
I teaspoon lemon juice
2 tablespoons horseradish
Chopped chives

Whip cream until stiff. Fold in sugar, lemon juice, and horseradish. Chill in serving dish for several hours. Sprinkle with chopped chives.

Makes about 2 cups

BULGUR PILAF

3 tablespoons margarine
¾ cup chopped celery
¾ cup sliced mushrooms
I ½ cups bulgur
3 cups chicken broth or beef bouillon
½ teaspoon dill weed
½ teaspoon oregano
¾ teaspoon salt
½ teaspoon pepper
I ½ tablespoons chopped parsley
3 tablespoons sliced pimientos

Melt margarine in deep saucepan. Add celery, mushrooms, and bulgur, and stir. Cook until tender but not brown. Add broth or bouillon, dill weed, oregano, salt, and pepper. Bring to boil, reduce heat, cover, and cook 15 minutes. Stir in parsley and pimientos.

May also add chopped pecans, chopped green pepper, sliced olives, or grated carrot.

Serves 8

TOMATO SCALLOP
An updated version of an old Virginia favorite

2 ½ cups canned tomatoes
I cup soft breadcrumbs
I tablespoon chopped onion
⅓ cup butter
I tablespoon flour
I tablespoon sugar
I teaspoon dry mustard
I teaspoon salt
½ teaspoon oregano
2 slices buttered bread, cubed for topping

Preheat oven to 350°.

Mix tomatoes, breadcrumbs, and onions in bowl.

Melt butter and add flour, sugar, mustard, salt, and oregano. Add to tomato mixture and mix well. Put into a small 7 x 11-inch casserole and cover with buttered bread cubes. May be doubled.

Bake about 1 hour.

Serves 4 to 6

ZESTY GREEN BEANS

1 pound small, tender whole green beans
2 teaspoons chopped parsley
1 ½ tablespoons red wine vinegar
1 ½ teaspoons Dijon mustard
⅓ cup olive oil
Black pepper to taste
1 small red onion, thinly sliced

▨ Cook green beans until barely tender. Drain and set aside. Whisk together parsley, vinegar, mustard, olive oil, and pepper.

▨ Place beans on serving dish and top with onion rings. Spoon vinaigrette over beans and onions. May be served hot or cold.

▨ Serves 8

SHERWOOD FOREST ORANGE CREAM SAUCE

2 egg yolks
½ cup sugar
½ cup orange juice
1 cup heavy cream, whipped

▨ Combine egg yolks, sugar, and orange juice, and cook until thick. When cool, add cream. Serve immediately on cake slices.

▨ Makes 2 cups

FRANCES'S ANGEL FOOD CAKE
*From the family recipe file of
President John Tyler's descendants*

1 cup sifted flour
1 ½ cups sugar, divided
1 ¾ cups (about 12) egg whites
2 teaspoons cream of tartar
¾ teaspoon salt
1 teaspoon vanilla
¼ teaspoon almond extract

▨ Sift flour and sugar separately. Add ½ cup sugar to flour and sift 3 times.

▨ Beat egg whites until frothy. Add cream of tartar and salt and continue beating until egg whites are stiff enough to hold shape. Add sugar gradually, beating thoroughly after each addition. Fold in flour, about ¼ cup at a time. Add vanilla and almond extract, and mix well.

▨ Pour into ungreased 10-inch tube pan and start in cold oven. Bake at 325° 45 minutes to 1 hour. Take out of oven and turn upside down. Leave in pan until thoroughly cooled, or cake will fall.

▨ Slice into serving portions and top with Sherwood Forest Orange Cream Sauce.

▨ Serves 24

BARTER THEATRE REVIEW PARTY
ABINGDON

"*T*he play's the thing!" Since colonial times, Virginians have always loved their theater. The Barter Theatre in Abingdon, the State Theater of Virginia, is America's longest running professional resident theater company. It was founded in 1933 during the Great Depression by an innovative (and hungry) young actor named Robert Porterfield. Faced with the trials of long unemployment, he proposed a novel idea: why not barter the talents of hungry actors for surplus produce? Living in empty buildings at nearby Martha Washington College and producing plays in the old Town Hall across the street, the company finished the first season with $4.35 in cash, two barrels of jelly, and a collective weight gain of about 300 pounds! Thus Barter Theatre was born.

When playwright Austin Strong accepted a country ham in lieu of a royalty payment, he began a tradition, with Noel Coward, Thornton Wilder, Robert Sherwood, and Maxwell Anderson following suit. Since that first shaky season, Barter has graduated a long list of celebrated alumni who got their start and early training there: Hume Cronyn, Patricia Neal, Gregory Peck, Ernest Borgnine, and David Birney, to name a few.

Barter teaches as well as entertains. In early spring, it presents four weeks of classic and contemporary drama selected for its educational as well as its theatrical value; up to 10,000 high school students and teachers attend these early-morning performances. In late May, the regular summer-fall season opens, and at the beginning of the year, the Barter tours, traveling throughout Virginia and into neighboring states. As always, since its inception, Barter's emphasis is on good theater well done, theater that is universal and relevant, entertaining, and enlightening. The thousands of people who flock to its performances attest to its ongoing success.

The small town of Abingdon (population about 7,000) is worth a look itself. The oldest town west of the Blue Ridge Mountains, it boasts lovely old homes neatly restored and a sprightly culture, alive with music, art, drama, crafts, antiques, and good food.

An exhilarating evening of theater calls for an encore afterward — no one wants the magic to stop. What better way to continue the play than a late supper with candlelight, lovely food, and animated conversation? We offer two menus, both made ahead to reach the table on cue. The cold, sauce-blanketed chicken, crisp snow-pea salad, and cooling orange slices are followed with a dramatic and luxurious grand finale of chocolate gâteau drizzled with Melba sauce, while the spicy kick of Shanghai beef curry is balanced by the chill of a salad and the sweetness of pineapple. Both provide great culinary theater for your guests:

the right combination of ingredients and inspiration. Expect curtain calls!

Though not a picture of a theater's "green room," the painting reproduced here and titled *The Green Room* conveys the anticipation actors must feel while awaiting their turn before the footlights. Through the restrained use of color, the half-open door, and the figure rather hazily defined in space, artist Felix Vallotton has depicted both energy and contemplation. The painting illustrates well the influence of the Nabis, a group of artists allied with the French Symbolist poets, to which Vallotton belonged. They held that the role of art was not to reproduce nature but to give expression to the artist's inner world.

Felix Vallotton (Swiss, 1865-1925), *The Green Room*, 1904, oil on board. Collection of the Virginia Museum of Fine Arts, Richmond. Collection of Mr. and Mrs. Paul Mellon.

COLD CHICKEN IN A BLANKET
The sauce serves as the blanket.

2 5-pound roasting chickens
1 ½ cups chicken broth or canned
   consommé to cover chickens
6 whole carrots
4 stalks celery
4 white onions
4 tablespoons butter or margarine
4 tablespoons flour
½ cup heavy cream
Zest of 1 lemon
Salt
Pepper
½ teaspoon mace
1 scant tablespoon lemon juice
2 egg yolks, beaten
Snow peas, bacon curls, or parsley
   for garnish

Place chickens in large pot and cover with broth. Add carrots, celery, and onions. Cover and simmer gently until tender. Remove from heat and let cool in broth. Reserve broth and carrots. Skin chicken and remove all meat in the largest pieces possible.

Melt butter or margarine and add flour. Cook gently over low heat, blending well, one minute. Warm 1 ½ cups broth with cream and add to mixture of butter and flour. Add lemon zest, salt, pepper, and mace. Gradually add lemon juice after sauce has thickened.

Pour a little sauce into beaten egg yolks. Then pour egg yolk mixture back into sauce and cook briefly.

Dip chicken pieces in sauce and arrange on platter with white meat in the center and dark meat around the white. Touch up with additional sauce when needed. Refrigerate.

At serving time, garnish with the cooked carrots and blanched, chilled snow peas if available. Crispy bacon curls and parsley can also be used to garnish.

Serves 10 to 12

WILD RICE SALAD

Dressing:
  I teaspoon honey
  I teaspoon salt
  ¾ cup olive oil
  ¾ cup vegetable oil
  ¼ cup vinegar
  ¼ cup dry sherry
  I clove garlic, crushed

  3 cups cooked (¾ cup raw) wild rice
  2 tablespoons scallions, sliced
  I cup frozen green peas, thawed
  10 cherry tomatoes, halved
  I cup artichoke hearts, quartered
  ½ cup dressing
  ½ cup chopped parsley
  Salt and pepper to taste
  Parsley sprigs for garnish

To make dressing, mix honey and salt in blender. Add oils and vinegar alternately until thick. Slowly drip in sherry.

Add garlic and store in jar in refrigerator. May also be used on mixed greens.

To make salad, mix together wild rice, scallions, peas, 8 tomato halves, artichoke hearts, ½ cup dressing, and parsley, and toss lightly. Correct seasoning and serve at room temperature. Garnish with 2 tomato halves and sprigs of parsley.

Serves 10

SESAME SNOW PEAS

½ pound snow peas, trimmed and
  blanched 30 seconds
½ pound mushrooms, sliced
Lettuce or radicchio

Dressing:
  I tablespoon vinegar
  I tablespoon sugar
  I garlic clove, minced
  ¾ teaspoon salt
  I tablespoon lemon juice
  ⅓ cup vegetable oil
  2 tablespoons sesame seeds, lightly toasted

Mix vinegar, sugar, garlic, salt, and lemon juice. Slowly add oil and whisk. Stir in sesame seeds.

Line a shallow bowl with lettuce and radicchio for color. Pile peas and mushrooms in center and pour dressing over all.

Serves 8

SPICY ORANGE SLICES

8 even-sized, unpeeled navel oranges
4 cups sugar
1 cup white vinegar
½ cup water
10 whole cloves
2 cinnamon sticks

Discard end pieces of oranges and slice into ¼-inch-thick slices. Cover with water and simmer covered 45 minutes to 1 hour until tender. Do not boil. Drain carefully.

Boil sugar, vinegar, ½ cup water, cloves, and cinnamon sticks 5 minutes. Carefully add orange slices and simmer, uncovered, 45 minutes, or until oranges are well glazed. Do not boil.

Transfer slices carefully into sterilized jars, stacking evenly. Fill jars with hot syrup, distributing spices. Seal.

Refrigerate before serving. Serve with chicken, turkey, duck, goose, or venison.

Makes 3 ½ pints

CHOCOLATE GÂTEAU WITH MELBA SAUCE

4 eggs, separated
4 4-ounce bars German sweet chocolate
½ cup unsalted butter, softened
4 teaspoons sugar
4 teaspoons flour

Melba sauce:
  1 cup (about 1 pint) raspberries
  ½ cup currant jelly
  1 tablespoon cornstarch
  ⅛ teaspoon salt
  ½ cup sugar
  3 tablespoons brandy

Preheat oven to 425°.

Lightly grease 9 x 5 x 3-inch loaf pan and line with wax paper. Allow separated eggs to reach room temperature.

In top of double boiler, melt chocolate over hot, not boiling, water. Remove and beat in butter with spoon.

With portable hand mixer, beat egg whites until stiff. Set aside. With same beaters, beat egg yolks until thick and lemon colored. Slowly add sugar, beating constantly. Add flour, beating just until blended. Stir into chocolate mixture.

With rubber spatula or wire whisk, fold egg whites into chocolate mixture. Pour into prepared pan. Reduce oven temperature to 350°. Bake 25 minutes. Let cool completely on wire rack. Cake will fall like a cheesecake. Wrap well and refrigerate overnight.

Remove from pan by putting hot cloths on bottom of pan to loosen. Remove wax paper. Slice and serve on plate spread with Melba sauce. Keep leftover gâteau in refrigerator well wrapped.

To make Melba sauce, mash berries through sieve to remove seeds. Bring jelly and berry purée to a boil in saucepan. Mix cornstarch, salt, and sugar, and dissolve in brandy. Add to berry mixture and cook until thick and clear. Cool. May be frozen.

Serves 12

SHANGHAI BEEF CURRY

1 ½ pounds round steak, trimmed and
    cubed
1 cup chopped onion
2 tablespoons butter or margarine
2 ¼ cups water, divided
1 tablespoon sugar
1 teaspoon salt
3 tablespoons grated coconut
1 tablespoon curry powder or to taste
2 tablespoons flour
Condiments: chutney, coconut, grape jelly,
    ground peanuts, currants, and grated
    sharp cheddar cheese

In large skillet, brown steak and onions in
butter. Add 2 cups water, sugar, salt, coconut,
and curry powder. Simmer 1 hour.

Mix flour and ¼ cup water to a smooth
paste and add to skillet. Mix in well and allow
sauce to thicken.

Serve over rice with condiments.

Serves 4 to 6

ETTA'S SALAD

½ cup sliced almonds
3 tablespoons sugar
½ head iceberg lettuce
½ head romaine lettuce
1 cup chopped celery
2 spring onions, chopped
1 11-ounce can mandarin oranges

Dressing:
½ teaspoon salt
¼ teaspoon pepper
¼ cup vegetable oil
1 tablespoon chopped parsley
2 tablespoons sugar
2 tablespoons vinegar
Dash Tabasco

Combine almonds and sugar and cook over
medium heat until nuts are coated. Quickly
lift out onto wax paper and cool.

To make dressing, mix ingredients together
and chill.

At serving time, mix salad ingredients, add
almonds, and toss with dressing.

Serves 4 to 6

PINEAPPLE VICTORIA

1 cup sugar
⅓ cup water
¼ cup Grand Marnier or Triple Sec liqueur
Zest of 1 orange
¼ cup lime juice
2 fresh pineapples, cut into chunks

Boil sugar and water 1 minute. Add liqueur,
orange zest, and lime juice. Pour over pineapple chunks and let marinate at least 1 hour.

Serve cold for dessert.

Serves 8

Extra Recipes

APPETIZERS

SHRIMP SPREAD APPETIZER

2 8-ounce packages cream cheese, softened
2 teaspoons horseradish
1 12-ounce jar cocktail sauce
1 ½ cups (about 1 pound) baby cooked shrimp
⅓ cup chopped green onion
⅓ cup chopped green pepper
⅓ cup sliced ripe olives
⅓ cup diced fresh tomatoes, drained
½ cup freshly grated Parmesan cheese

Combine softened cream cheese and horseradish until smooth. Spread mixture evenly on large, decorative plate.

Spread cocktail sauce on top of cream cheese mixture. Arrange shrimp evenly on cocktail sauce, then spread onion, pepper, olives, and tomatoes evenly on top.

Sprinkle Parmesan cheese on last. Refrigerate until serving time. Serve with crackers.

Serves 12 to 15

HOT CLAM SPREAD
A quick and easy spread or dip

4 6 ½-ounce cans minced clams with juice
1 cup seasoned breadcrumbs
½ pound butter, melted
1 teaspoon dried parsley
1 teaspoon dried oregano
Dash garlic salt
Dash salt and pepper
Hot pepper sauce to taste
8 ounces mozzarella cheese, shredded
1 cup Parmesan cheese

Preheat oven to 350°.

Combine clams, breadcrumbs, butter, parsley, oregano, garlic salt, salt and pepper, hot sauce, and mozzarella.

Put in 9-inch ovenproof dish. Sprinkle with Parmesan and bake 15 to 30 minutes, or until hot and bubbly. Serve with crackers.

Serves 15 to 20

ARTICHOKE APPETIZER
Appealing even before you dig in

Juice of 1 lemon
4 medium artichokes

Dipping sauce:
    2 3-ounce packages cream cheese, softened
    Few drops fresh-pressed garlic juice
    ¼ cup sour cream
    2 teaspoons wine vinegar
    ¼ cup minced ripe olives
    Salt to taste

Fill bowl with water to cover artichokes. Add lemon juice. With scissors, trim off thorny tip of each leaf and drop into lemon water to prevent discoloring.

Bring salted water to a boil and drop in drained artichokes. Cook 30 minutes or until tender. Drain and chill. Just before serving, remove leaves from each artichoke.

To make sauce, blend cream cheese, garlic juice, sour cream, vinegar, olives, and salt. Chill.

To serve, layer leaves on a platter, leaving room for sauce bowl in center.

Serves 16 to 20

HOLIDAY CAVIAR

1 8-ounce tub whipped cream cheese
1 6 ½-ounce jar red lumpfish
½ teaspoon lemon juice
½ teaspoon minced onion

Gently mix cream cheese, lumpfish, lemon juice, and onion. Chill. Serve with bland crackers.

Serves 16 to 20

MARTINI OLIVES

2 cups green olives with liquid
1 cup wine vinegar
3 cloves garlic, minced
Diced rind and juice of 1 lemon

Mix olives, vinegar, garlic, and lemon rind and juice in quart jar. Seal tightly and refrigerate 2 days before serving.

LIVER PATE

1 pound bacon
1 pound chicken livers
2 eggs, hard boiled
6 green onions, sliced
Garlic salt or seasoned salt to
    taste
Mayonnaise to bind

❖ Cook bacon until crisp. Remove and drain well, reserving the drippings. Add livers and cook until done.

❖ Put livers, eggs, onions, and seasoning in food processor and blend until smooth. Add enough mayonnaise to make a spread.

❖ Remove from processor and add crumbled bacon. Add more mayonnaise if needed and stir well.

❖ Place in bowl or mold and chill. Serve with bland crackers.

❖ Makes 2 ½ cups

PEPPY SHRIMP RING
*Good for an
entrée or a cocktail party*

2 envelopes unflavored gelatin
½ cup cold water
1 ½ teaspoons salt (optional)
¼ cup ketchup
2 cups sour cream
¼ cup lemon juice
¼ cup horseradish
3 cups (about 1 ½ pounds)
    cooked, cleaned shrimp, cut in
    pieces
1 cup chopped green pepper
1 cup chopped celery

❖ Soften gelatin in cold water, dissolve over hot water, and cool.

❖ Combine salt, ketchup, sour cream, lemon juice, and horseradish, and add to gelatin. Add shrimp, green pepper, and celery. Mix well and pour into 5-cup ring mold. Chill until firm.

❖ Serves 6

COAST SHRIMP

1 pound shrimp, cooked and
    cleaned
2 medium onions, cut into rings
¼ of 3 ½-ounce bottle capers
3 to 4 bay leaves

Marinade:
    1 cup salad oil
    ½ teaspoon dry mustard
    Dash red pepper
    ⅓ cup ketchup
    1 teaspoon salt
    1 teaspoon sugar
    2 tablespoons Worcestershire
        sauce
    Dash Tabasco sauce
    ⅓ cup vinegar
    1 clove garlic

❖ To make marinade, combine all ingredients and pour over shrimp and onions. Marinate 24 hours in refrigerator. Turn several times.

❖ Layer shrimp, onions, capers, and bay leaves into jar with tight-fitting cap.

❖ Drain and place in bowl. Use picks to serve. Will keep in marinade in refrigerator several days.

❖ Serves 16 to 20

EMILY'S CLAM DIP

10 strips bacon, cooked and
    crumbled, reserving drippings
3 6 ½-ounce cans minced clams,
    drained
6 cloves garlic, pressed
3 teaspoons dried basil
4 teaspoons cornstarch
2 10 ½-ounce cans tomato purée,
    divided
1 ½ teaspoons salt
¾ teaspoon pepper
5 tablespoons minced parsley
6 tablespoons Parmesan cheese

❖ Measure 6 tablespoons bacon drippings in skillet and heat. Add clams, garlic, and basil.

❖ Dissolve cornstarch in ½ cup tomato purée. Add to skillet with remaining purée, salt, pepper, and parsley. Bring to a boil, reduce heat, and cook until thickened, stirring slowly. Add Parmesan and blend.

❖ Serve from chafing dish with corn chips .

❖ Makes 3 ½ cups

Soups

Heavenly Tomato Soup

1 6-ounce can tomato paste
3 cups chicken broth or stock
2 to 3 medium tomatoes, peeled and coarsely diced
1 1 ¼-ounce package onion soup mix (optional)
1 3-ounce package cream cheese, cubed
1 to 2 stalks chives or scallions with tops for garnish
Sherry to taste

❈ Combine tomato paste, broth, and tomatoes, and boil for about 3 minutes.

❈ If using onion soup mix, add to stock mixture.

❈ Add cream cheese, remove from heat, stir gently until cheese gets very soft.

❈ Ladle into bowls and garnish with slices of chives or scallions. A teaspoon of sherry per bowl may also be added.

❈ Serves 6

Baked Brie Soup
A Virginia Museum Dining Room favorite

1 pound sliced mushrooms
3 tablespoons butter
¼ cup flour
3 cups fresh chicken stock
1 cup white wine
2 cups half-and-half
Salt and white pepper to taste
1 pound Brie cheese

❈ Preheat broiler.

❈ Sauté mushrooms in butter until soft, stir in flour and gradually add stock and wine. Simmer 15 minutes, stirring often. Add half-and-half and salt and pepper to taste.

❈ Ladle into 8 ovenproof bowls or soup crocks. Slice Brie and place on top of soup. Broil 8 inches from heat until bubbly.

❈ Serve with a lusty salad and French bread.

❈ Serves 8

Basque Potato Soup

1 pound smoked sausage, sliced in rounds
1 cup chopped onion
2 1-pound cans tomatoes with juice
2 cups water
2 beef bouillon cubes
1 bay leaf
½ teaspoon thyme
6 potatoes, pared and diced
1 cup celery, sliced diagonally
2 tablespoons chopped celery leaves
2 carrots, cut in rounds
Shredded cabbage (optional)
½ cup red wine (optional)
1 tablespoon lemon juice
Salt and pepper to taste

❈ Brown sausage and onion in a large pot or Dutch oven, about 5 minutes. Add tomatoes, water, bouillon cubes, bay leaf, and thyme. Cover and cook about 15 minutes.

❈ Add potatoes, celery, celery leaves, and carrots, and simmer 40 minutes. Shredded cabbage may be added for last 20 minutes, if desired. Red wine added during cooking adds to the flavor.

❈ Before serving, add lemon juice and salt and pepper to taste. Good with French bread and salad.

❈ Serves 6 generously

Meatball Minestrone Soup
Just the thing for a cold winter night

2 ½ pounds extra-lean ground
    beef
2 cups chopped onion, divided
5 tablespoons instant beef bouil-
    lon granules, divided
8 cups water
2 16-ounce cans stewed tomatoes
1 ½ teaspoons dried thyme
¼ teaspoon pepper
2 cups shredded cabbage
4 ounces thin spaghetti,
    broken into small pieces
Parmesan cheese
Fresh parsley for garnish

❧ Preheat oven to 350°.

❧ Combine beef, 1 cup chopped
onion, and 2 tablespoons beef bouillon. Mix well, shape into ½-inch
meatballs, place in shallow pan with
sides to catch the grease, and bake
18 to 20 minutes. Remove from
oven, drain well, and set aside.

❧ In 6-quart Dutch oven, combine
meatballs, water, tomatoes with
juice, remaining bouillon granules,
thyme, and pepper. Cover, bring to a
boil, then reduce heat, and simmer 1
hour. Add cabbage and spaghetti
and cook 15 more minutes. Serve
with Parmesan cheese and parsley.

❧ Serves 12

Fresh Fruit Soup

4 tablespoons quick tapioca
4 tablespoons sugar
5 cups water, divided
1 12-ounce can frozen peach-
    orange or orange juice
6 cups fresh fruit: grapes, peaches,
    melon, bananas, plums, or
    strawberries
2 tablespoons lemon juice

❧ Combine tapioca, sugar, and 2
cups water. Bring to a rolling boil,
stirring constantly to ensure tapioca
dissolves completely. Remove from
heat and add frozen juice, stirring
until melted. Add remaining 3 cups
water. Cool 20 minutes, stir, cover,
and chill.

❧ Cut fruit into bite-size pieces, and
when soup is chilled, add fruit and
lemon juice.

❧ Serves 12

Lentil Stew
Hearty, healthy, and good, too

2 large onions, chopped
2 medium carrots, scraped and
    chopped
1 cup dry lentils
½ cup chopped fresh parsley
1 16-ounce can whole tomatoes,
    undrained and coarsely
    chopped
3 cups chicken broth
¼ cup dry sherry
½ teaspoon dried whole thyme
½ teaspoon dried whole
    marjoram
½ teaspoon pepper

❧ Combine all ingredients in Dutch
oven, bring to a boil, cover, reduce
heat, and simmer 45 minutes, or
until lentils are tender.

❧ Makes 8 ½ cups

Oyster Stew

½ pint whole milk or
    half-and-half
½ stick butter
1 teaspoon Worcestershire sauce
1 pint oysters with their liquid
Salt and pepper to taste

❧ Put milk, butter, and Worcestershire sauce in medium saucepan and
heat until ingredients are steaming.
Do not scald milk.

❧ Add oysters and liquid and, slowly
stirring constantly, continue to heat
until oysters curl and the stew is very
hot. Do not allow to boil.

❧ Add salt and pepper to taste and
serve in warmed bowls.

❧ Serves 2

CHEESE AND EGGS

SUNRISE SURPRISE

I medium tomato
Salt and pepper to taste
2 eggs
I teaspoon butter
I tablespoon grated Parmesan
    cheese
Fresh parsley for garnish

Preheat oven to 350°.

Peel tomato and quarter it, but do
not separate sections.

Place tomato in greased, 4-inch
oven-proof container. Salt and pepper to taste.

Crack 2 eggs into center of tomato.

Top with butter and cheese and
bake until whites of eggs are set and
yolks are desired consistency, about
15 to 20 minutes.

Garnish with parsley.

Serves I

CHEESE GRITS
A new twist to an old favorite!

I ½ cups quick grits
6 cups water
I pound grated extra-sharp
    cheddar cheese
I ½ sticks butter or margarine
3 eggs, beaten
2 tablespoons Lawry's salt

Preheat oven to 350°.

Cook grits according to the directions on the box, omitting salt. Add
cheese, margarine, eggs, and seasoned salt. Mix thoroughly. Pour in
rectangular 3-quart casserole. Bake I
hour.

Serves 8

GÂTEAU FROMAGE
A simple but delicious cheese pie

2 cups grated cheddar cheese
I egg, beaten
I tablespoon flour
I scant cup milk
I unbaked deep-dish pie shell

Preheat oven to 450°.

Place cheese evenly in pie shell.
Mix egg, flour, and milk, and pour
over the cheese. Jiggle pie pan a bit
to mix.

Bake 25 to 30 minutes. Let sit a
few minutes until it will cut neatly
but is still hot. May also add onions,
ham, bacon, shrimp, and/or vegetables.

Serves 6

APPLE PANLETS
A combination omelette and pancake

4 tablespoons margarine
4 eggs
I teaspoon salt
¼ cup sugar
I cup all-purpose flour
I ⅓ cups milk
I teaspoon grated lemon peel
2 tablespoons lemon juice
2 apples, peeled, quartered,
    and cored
½ to I cup sour cream
powdered sugar

Preheat oven to 450°.

Melt margarine in a 9 x 13-inch
glass baking dish in oven. Place eggs,
salt, sugar, flour, milk, lemon peel,
and lemon juice in food processor.
Mix until smooth. Add apples. Turn
processor on and off several times
for a few seconds. Apples should
remain coarse.

Spread melted margarine evenly in
pan. Pour batter into pan and bake
12-15 minutes, until puffed and del-
icately browned. Spread with sour
cream and powdered sugar. Cut into
squares.

Serves 4-6

POULTRY AND GAME

ORANGE GLAZED CHICKEN
Elegant, quick, and easy

4 chicken breasts, skinned, boned,
　and split
1 stick butter
4 green onions, chopped
1 6-ounce can frozen orange juice
½ cup golden raisins
½ cup slivered almonds

Sauté chicken in butter until golden brown.

Add onions and orange juice, and simmer 30 minutes.

Sprinkle with raisins and almonds and cook 5 minutes more before serving.

Serves 8

CHICKEN CURRY
*Something different for those
who love curry*

2 cloves garlic, minced
2 medium onions, chopped
½ cup melted butter
1 tablespoon flour
1 tablespoon curry powder
1 tablespoon sugar
½ teaspoon dry mustard
1 cup tomato purée
1 20-ounce can apple pie filling
2 cups chicken broth
Rind and juice of 1 lime
2 whole uncooked chicken breasts,
　boned and cubed
1 cup raisins
½ cup cream
2 tablespoons chopped chutney
Condiments: cooked bacon,
　chopped green onion, salted
　peanuts, grated boiled eggs

Sauté garlic and onions in butter. Add flour, curry, sugar, and mustard, and mix well.

Add purée, apples, broth, lime rind and juice, chicken, and raisins. Simmer 30 minutes. Reduce heat and add cream and chutney. Cook on low 15 more minutes.

Serve over rice with condiments.

Serves 4 to 6

THAI STIR-FRY

1 pound uncooked chicken
　breasts, cut into strips
¼ cup soy sauce, divided
1 clove garlic, minced
½ teaspoon red pepper flakes
¼ cup peanut butter
2 tablespoons vegetable oil,
　divided
3 tablespoons brown sugar
¼ cup diced onion
½ cup diced red sweet pepper
2 cups shredded cabbage

Marinate chicken in 5 tablespoons soy sauce, garlic, and pepper flakes for 3 hours.

Combine peanut butter, 1 tablespoon oil, sugar and remaining soy sauce; reserve.

Stir-fry chicken in remaining oil, and add onion and pepper. Stir in cabbage and peanut sauce. Cover, reduce heat, and simmer until cabbage is soft.

Serves 4

GOLDEN CHICKEN

⅔ cup olive oil
Salt and pepper
3 whole chicken breasts, halved
6 chicken legs
6 chicken thighs
1½ cup dry white wine
¾ cup sliced fresh mushrooms
⅓ cup chopped shallots
1 ½ cups pitted black olives
3 cups chopped fresh or canned
　tomatoes

Preheat oven to 350°.

Heat oil to 375° in large skillet. Lightly salt and pepper chicken pieces and brown in skillet. Remove and place in large casserole. Pour off skillet oil and reserve. Deglaze pan with wine and pour over chicken. Return reserved oil to skillet and sauté mushrooms and shallots until limp. Add to casserole with olives and tomatoes. Bake 45 minutes.

Serves 6 to 8

ROAST ROCK CORNISH GAME HENS

¾ cup butter
¾ cup dry white wine
3 tablespoons dried tarragon, divided
6 Cornish hens
6 cloves garlic
Salt and pepper
Garlic salt

In saucepan, melt butter, add wine, and 1 tablespoon tarragon. In each hen, place 1 clove garlic, 1 teaspoon tarragon, ¼ teaspoon salt, and ⅛ teaspoon pepper. Sprinkle outside liberally with garlic salt. Refrigerate at least 1 hour.

Heat oven to 425°. Roast hens in large shallow open pan for about 1 hour, basting often with pan juices.

Serves 6

BRAISED DOVES
Long, slow cooking makes these a success.

8 doves, cleaned
Salt and pepper
1 stick butter or margarine
½ cup red wine
½ cup water

Split birds down back. Salt and pepper both sides.

Melt butter in frying pan or electric skillet and sauté birds on both sides until golden brown. Add wine and water and boil slowly 1 minute. Turn heat to low, cover, and simmer 2 hours, turning often. Add more butter, wine, and water if needed.

Serves 4

BAKED WILD DUCK

4 wild ducks, ready for baking
1 24-ounce bottle Italian salad dressing
Salt and pepper
4 apples, quartered
4 large oranges, cut in chunks
1 fresh pineapple, cut in chunks

Marinate ducks in dressing overnight. Remove from marinade and salt and pepper inside and out. Stuff cavities with apples, oranges, and pineapple.

Preheat oven to 300°.

Place ducks, breast side up, in roasting pan and cover tightly with aluminum foil. Bake 3 hours. Remove foil and broil until lightly browned.

Serves 8

ROAST GOOSE
Try this instead of turkey.

1 10- to 12-pound young goose
½ lemon
2 teaspoons salt
½ teaspoon pepper
5 apples, cored and quartered
20 pitted prunes
2 cups chicken bouillon
1 tablespoon cornstarch
¼ cup water

Preheat oven to 350°.

Clean goose, wipe thoroughly, and singe to remove pin feathers. Rub inside and out with lemon, salt, and pepper. Stuff cavity with apples and prunes. Secure with skewers and truss goose. Roast uncovered on rack in roasting pan, breast side up, until tender, about 2 ½ hours. Pour off fat during roasting. When almost done, leave oven door slightly open to make skin brittle.

Remove goose to hot platter and keep warm. To make gravy, pour bouillon in roasting pan and stir up browned pan bits. Strain pan juices. Skim off fat and pour pan drippings into saucepan. Mix cornstarch and water and stir into drippings. Simmer 5 minutes and adjust seasonings. Serve in gravy boat.

Serves 8

MEATS

FILET MIGNON

6 1-inch-thick fillets
2 tablespoons butter
12 large mushrooms, stems
    reserved and chopped
¼ cup chopped green onions
2 teaspoons cornstarch
1 cup red wine
½ cup water
2 tablespoons fresh parsley
Ground pepper
Salt

❈ Brown fillets on both sides over medium heat in butter. Place each on a square of heavy foil.

❈ Cook chopped mushroom stems and onions in butter remaining in pan. Blend in cornstarch and add wine, water, parsley, pepper, and salt. Cook until thickened. Spoon 2 tablespoons sauce over each fillet and top with 2 mushroom caps. Bring sides of foil over the meat, leaving a 1 ½-inch opening. Pinch the corners. Refrigerate until 30 minutes before serving.

❈ Preheat oven to 500°.

❈ Bake 15 to 20 minutes for rare. Reheat and serve any remaining sauce.

❈ Serves 6

LIZA'S MEATBALLS

1 pound ground beef
½ cup chopped fresh broccoli
⅓ cup cottage cheese
¼ cup Parmesan cheese
1 egg, beaten
¼ cup ketchup
½ teaspoon celery salt
Pepper
Oil for browning
2 cups beef broth
1 cup red wine

❈ Mix beef, broccoli, cottage cheese, Parmesan cheese, egg, ketchup, celery salt, and pepper. Form into balls.

❈ At this point, meatballs may be frozen on baking sheet, then stored in freezer in plastic bag.

❈ To cook, brown in skillet. Pour off excess fat. Add broth and wine. Simmer until meat is done.

❈ Serve over linguine. May also be used as cocktail meatballs.

BUTTERFLIED
LEG OF LAMB WITH PESTO

1 ½ cups olive oil, divided
6 cloves garlic, divided
3 ounces blanched almonds
3 cups fresh basil leaves
½ teaspoon salt
¼ teaspoon freshly ground
    pepper
1 6- to 7-pound leg of lamb,
    boned and butterflied
1 cup red wine

❈ Trim fell and all visible fat from lamb.

❈ Make pesto by placing ½ cup olive oil, 4 cloves garlic, and almonds in food processor fitted with metal blade. Process until fine. Add basil, salt, and pepper, and process until smooth.

❈ Cut small slits in lamb and stuff small amounts (½ teaspoon) pesto into slits. Repeat all over both sides of lamb. Combine remaining oil, red wine, and remaining garlic. Place lamb in glass dish and pour marinade over lamb. Marinate refrigerated up to 24 hours.

❈ Grill over medium-hot coals 25 minutes per side for medium rare, or until desired doneness.

❈ Serves 8

VEAL SCALLOPS
WITH LEMON ZEST

1 ½ cups fine bread crumbs
1 cup grated Parmesan cheese
Zest of 2 ½ lemons
1 teaspoon salt
⅛ teaspoon pepper
Veal scallops – allow 2 or 3
    per person
Flour for dredging
2 eggs, beaten
Oil for sautéing
Wedges of lemon for garnish

❈ Combine bread crumbs, cheese, lemon zest, salt, and pepper.

❈ Dredge veal in flour then dip in beaten eggs. Roll veal in crumb mixture.

❈ Sauté veal in small amount of vegetable oil until golden brown on each side – about 3 minutes per side. Drain on paper towels and serve with wedges of lemon.

❈ Measure out the amount of crumb mixture needed for number of scallops. The unused portion will keep in refrigerator if lightly covered.

Seafood

Petit Gratin de Crab au Vin Blanc

3 tablespoons butter, divided
2 tablespoons minced shallots or scallions
½ pound crabmeat
¼ teaspoon salt
⅛ teaspoon pepper
¼ teaspoon tarragon
⅓ cup dry vermouth
1 tablespoon cornstarch
¾ cup heavy cream, divided
½ teaspoon tomato paste
Salt, pepper, and lemon juice to taste
2 tablespoons grated Swiss cheese

❊ Preheat oven to 400°.

❊ Using 8-inch nonstick skillet, melt 2 tablespoons butter. Stir in shallots or scallions and cook until tender. Stir in crabmeat, sprinkle with salt, pepper, and tarragon. Cook, stirring 1 to 2 minutes, then pour in vermouth. Raise heat and boil, stirring until liquid has almost evaporated. Remove from heat.

❊ Beat cornstarch and 2 to 3 tablespoons cream to make paste. Gradually add 4 more tablespoons cream and tomato paste. Stir mixture into crabmeat and simmer until thick, stirring often. Add salt, pepper, and lemon juice to taste.

❊ Spoon crabmeat mixture into lightly buttered shells or ramekins. Sprinkle with cheese and 1 tablespoon melted butter. Refrigerate if not served immediately.

❊ To heat, brown cheese in upper third of oven about 15 minutes.

❊ Serves 4

Baked Oysters and Mushroom Parmesan

6 tablespoons butter
1 pound sliced mushrooms
1 cup chopped onion
2 teaspoons chopped garlic
1 quart oysters, drained and liquid reserved
½ cup oyster liquid
4 tablespoons flour
2 tablespoons meat extract
Salt and pepper to taste
¾ cup fresh breadcrumbs
⅓ cup minced fresh parsley
⅓ cup grated Parmesan cheese
6 to 8 thin lemon slices

❊ Preheat oven to 400°.

❊ In a 12-inch sauté pan, melt 4 tablespoons butter. Add mushrooms and onion. Cover and simmer 10 minutes.

❊ Add garlic and oyster liquid and heat through. Add oysters and simmer until edges curl. Remove oysters, mushrooms, and onions with slotted spoon and place in a 1 ½ quart casserole dish or 8 individual baking dishes or shells.

❊ Make a thin paste by slowly adding part of the pan juices to the flour, stirring until smooth. Remove this mixture to pan, and whisk constantly until thickened. Add meat extract, salt, and pepper to taste.

❊ Add the sauce to the casserole or divide among the individual baking dishes.

❊ Mix together the crumbs, parsley, and cheese, and sprinkle on top. Dot with 2 tablespoons butter, and top with lemon slices.

❊ Bake 10 minutes or until bubbly.

❊ Serves 8

CRAB SUPREME
Hot or cold, it's delicious.

I pound crabmeat
½ cup mayonnaise
I tablespoon lemon juice
I tablespoon Worcestershire sauce
½ teaspoon onion powder
Butter at room temperature
Parsley sprigs or minced parsley
    for garnish

Preheat oven to 350°.

Pick over crabmeat and remove shells and cartilage.

Mix crabmeat, mayonnaise, lemon juice, Worcestershire sauce, and onion powder.

Spoon mixture into 4 seafood baking shells, dividing evenly. Dot each with butter.

Bake 10 to 15 minutes or until bubbly hot. Garnish with parsley.

Mixture may be chilled, omitting butter, and served in avocado halves, in hollowed-out tomatoes, or just on lettuce leaves.

Serves 4

CORN AND OYSTER CASSEROLE
A holiday favorite

I quart oysters, drained and
    coarsely chopped
40 ounces cream-style corn
½ cup light cream or evaporated
    milk
I teaspoon salt
½ teaspoon pepper
Dash hot pepper sauce
2 ½ to 3 cups coarsely crumbled
    saltine crackers
I cup melted butter

Preheat oven to 350°.

Mix oysters with corn, cream, salt, pepper, and hot pepper sauce.

Add cracker crumbs to butter. Layer with other ingredients in low-sided, oblong, ovenproof casserole and bake 40 minutes.

Serves 8 to 10

BAKED FISH FILLET WITH MUSTARD SAUCE

I tablespoon Dijon mustard
2 dashes Worcestershire sauce
Splash white wine
Grated Swiss cheese
Fillets of trout, flounder, spot,
    or other fish

Preheat oven to 350°.

Mix mustard, Worcestershire sauce, and white wine. Spread mixture on fillets and bake 12 minutes.

Remove from oven, sprinkle Swiss cheese to cover fillets and return to oven for 3 minutes. Increase recipe as needed for the number of fillets you have to cook.

Serves I

SAUTEED SHAD ROE WITH SMITHFIELD HAM
A traditional Virginia favorite

2 sets shad roe
¼ cup all-purpose flour
Salt and pepper
2 tablespoons butter
2 ounces (4 to 8 very thin slices)
    Smithfield ham
I tablespoon lemon juice

Gently rinse shad roe in bowl of cold water. Dry on paper towel. Separate pairs of roe carefully so membrane is not broken. Dust shad roe with flour and sprinkle with salt and pepper.

Melt butter in skillet over low heat. Add shad roe, cover, and cook over low heat 8 to 10 minutes, turning once. Roe will be slightly golden on outside and slightly soft to the touch. (By cooking slowly, eggs will not pop.)

Place set of roe on each plate. Keep warm. Put ham in skillet and cook until heated, add lemon juice, spoon over roe and serve.

Serves 2 to 4

VEGETABLES

CREAMED CELERY WITH PECANS
A very different vegetable

2 tablespoons chopped onion
¼ cup plus 2 tablespoons butter, divided
5 cups celery, cut in I-inch pieces
Water to cover
¼ cup flour
2 cups milk
I teaspoon salt
⅛ teaspoon pepper
½ cup heavy cream
¾ cups coarsely chopped pecans
⅓ cup breadcrumbs

❁ Preheat oven to 375°.

❁ Sauté onion in ¼ cup butter until tender. Cook celery in water until tender-crisp, 10 to 15 minutes. Drain.

❁ Add flour to onion and butter. Cook until flour is a light golden color. Stir in milk, salt, pepper, and cream. Cook until thick.

❁ Add celery and put in 2-quart casserole. Sprinkle pecans on top. Melt 2 tablespoons butter, add breadcrumbs, and mix well. Spread over pecans. Bake 15 minutes or until brown.

❁ Serves 8

BLACK-EYED PEA CAKES

I tablespoon butter
¾ cup finely chopped red onion
½ cup finely chopped sweet red pepper
I jalapeño pepper, finely chopped
2 16-ounce cans black-eyed peas, rinsed and drained
½ cup fine breadcrumbs
2 large egg yolks
¼ cup chopped fresh cilantro
I teaspoon cumin
I teaspoon thyme
I teaspoon oregano
½ teaspoon salt
I teaspoon dry mustard
3 cloves garlic, crushed
⅓ cup yellow cornmeal
¼ cup oil
¾ cup sour cream
¼ cup chopped green onion
I ½ cups tomato salsa

❁ Heat butter and sauté onion, red pepper, and jalapeño pepper. Cool slightly.

❁ In large bowl, mash peas to purée, add sautéed mixture, breadcrumbs, egg yolks, cilantro, cumin, thyme, oregano, salt, dry mustard, and garlic. Blend well. Divide into 12 portions and shape each into 2 ½-inch patty. Dip into cornmeal.

❁ Heat oil in skillet over medium high heat and cook patties 3 to 4 minutes on each side. Top each with I tablespoon sour cream and some green onion.

❁ Serve salsa on the side.

❁ Serves 6

RED CABBAGE AND APPLES

I ½ tablespoons butter
I small red cabbage, quartered and thinly sliced
I to 2 tart apples, grated
¼ cup vinegar
½ cup red currant jelly
½ teaspoon salt
¼ cup water
Pinch sugar

❁ Melt butter in heavy saucepan and add cabbage, apples, vinegar, jelly, salt, and water. Cover and simmer until cabbage is tender, about I hour, stirring occasionally. Add sugar and more salt if needed.

❁ Serve with pork or other meat dishes.

❁ Serves 4

KAYNE'S EGGPLANT

I medium eggplant, washed,
    unpeeled, and cut into
    ½-inch slices
I teaspoon sea salt
I cup fresh breadcrumbs
½ teaspoon garlic salt
¼ teaspoon freshly ground
    pepper
I tablespoon chopped fresh basil
    or ½ teaspoon dried
I tablespoon chopped fresh
    parsley or ½ teaspoon dried
I tablespoon chopped fresh
    marjoram or ½ teaspoon dried
I tablespoon chopped fresh
    oregano or ½ teaspoon dried
½ cup light mayonnaise

Preheat oven to 375°.

Place sliced eggplant on rack in
flat pan, sprinkle with salt, and let sit
20 minutes. Pat thoroughly dry with
paper towels. Mix breadcrumbs, garlic salt, pepper, and herbs. Coat eggplant with mayonnaise on both
sides. Dredge in crumb mixture.
Place on cookie sheet, not touching,
and bake 10 minutes. Turn over and
bake until tender. May be served
plain, with fresh tomato sauce, or
topped with sautéed veal scallop and
a slice of lemon.

Serves 4 to 6

ZESTY CARROTS
Horseradish gives it a zing.

6 to 8 carrots, peeled
2 tablespoons horseradish
2 tablespoons grated onion
½ cup mayonnaise
½ teaspoon salt
¼ teaspoon pepper
½ cup breadcrumbs
I tablespoon melted butter

Preheat oven 375°.

Cut carrots in lengthwise strips,
making them as thin as possible, like
shoestrings. Cook in small amount
of water until crispy tender. Drain
and place in shallow baking dish.
Mix horseradish, onion, mayonnaise,
salt, and pepper, and pour over carrots.

Toss breadcrumbs with butter and
sprinkle over carrots. Bake 15 to 20
minutes.

Serves 6 to 8

GRILLED ZUCCHINI WITH
BASIL BUTTER

½ cup softened butter
I garlic clove, minced
I tablespoon lemon juice
6 large fresh basil leaves snipped
    into small pieces
6 small to medium zucchini

To make basil butter, mash butter
with garlic, lemon juice, and basil in
small bowl.

Cut zucchini lengthwise in halves
and spread with basil butter.

Set aside at room temperature
until grill is hot.

Over medium fire, grill zucchini,
basting with basil butter frequently
and turning until tender, about 10
to 15 minutes. Top with smear of
remaining butter and serve at once.

Serves 6 to 8

DIJON POTATOES

8 to 12 (I ¼ to I ½ pounds)
    tiny new potatoes
3 tablespoons butter or margarine
I ½ tablespoons Dijon mustard
2 tablespoons finely chopped
    chives, green onion tops, or
    parsley

Peel a narrow layer of skin from
around the middle section of each
potato. Rinse potatoes. Place in a
shallow I ½-quart casserole. Cook
in microwave on High 12 to 14
minutes until potatoes are tender.

Mix butter, mustard, and chives,
and toss with hot potatoes. Serve
immediately.

Serves 4 to 6

SALADS

ZITI SALAD

1 16-ounce box ziti (large-cut pasta)
¼ cup milk
1 cup chopped purple onion
2 tomatoes, seeded and chopped
¾ cup chopped sweet pickle
1 cup chopped green peppers
1 ½ cups mayonnaise
½ cup sour cream
2 ½ teaspoons instant beef bouillon
½ teaspoon salt
½ teaspoon pepper
1 large shallot, minced
1 tablespoon sweet pickle juice
2 dashes wine vinegar
Chopped parsley for garnish

❧ Cook ziti according to directions on box. Drain and cool. Pour milk over ziti and toss. Add onion, tomatoes, pickle, and green pepper.

❧ Make dressing with mayonnaise, sour cream, and bouillon, stirring occasionally until bouillon is dissolved. Add to ziti mixture and toss well. Season with salt and pepper; add shallot, pickle juice, and wine vinegar. Toss well and chill in refrigerator several hours. Best made early in the day so flavors will develop. Garnish with chopped parsley.

❧ Serves 12 generously

CRUNCHY CHICKEN SALAD
A taste of India

2 cups mayonnaise, more if needed
2 to 3 teaspoons curry powder
4 ½ cups cooked, chopped chicken breast
4 cups cooked rice
½ to ¾ cups orange marmalade
1 4-ounce can crushed pineapple, drained
1 8-ounce can sliced water chestnuts, drained
1 ½ cups chopped celery
⅓ cup chutney
1 cup sliced, toasted almonds

❧ Mix mayonnaise and curry.

❧ Add remainder of ingredients except almonds. Mix well.

❧ Garnish with sliced almonds.

❧ Makes about 15 cups

SNOW-ON-THE-MOUNTAIN SALAD

1 bunch romaine lettuce
½ cup mayonnaise
2 tablespoons Parmesan cheese
1 tablespoon lemon juice
⅛ teaspoon garlic salt
Freshly ground pepper
¼ head cauliflower
4 strips bacon, crisply fried and crumbled
Crumbled blue cheese to taste
⅛ cup minced green onion tops

❧ Wash romaine and shake off excess water. Stack leaves and cut crosswise into small pieces. Transfer to salad bowl.

❧ Combine mayonnaise, Parmesan cheese, lemon juice, garlic salt, and a generous amount of pepper.

❧ Toss mayonnaise mixture with lettuce.

❧ Wash and trim cauliflower, then chop, using steel blade of food processor.

❧ Combine cauliflower, bacon, blue cheese, and green onions. Sprinkle over top of romaine salad. Serve as soon as possible. Tiny homemade croutons are another tasty addition.

❧ Serves 4

SHRIMP SALAD
Cauliflower adds the crunch.

1 ½ pounds medium-sized shrimp, cooked
2 cups cooked rice
¾ cup diced green pepper
1 7-ounce jar chopped pimiento
2 ½ cups diced cauliflower
6 sliced green onions
3 tablespoons sliced green olives
½ cup mayonnaise
Salt and pepper to taste

❧ Save 12 shrimp for garnish. Break remaining shrimp into large bowl. Add rice, green pepper, pimiento, cauliflower, onion, and olives. Stir in mayonnaise, salt, and pepper.

❧ Refrigerate overnight, tightly covered. Correct seasoning before serving.

❧ Serves 12

APPLE BLUE CHEESE SALAD
Quick and tasty

¼ very tart apple, cored and
  thinly sliced
Mixed salad greens
I tablespoon blue cheese
5 pecan halves, toasted and
  broken into pieces

❧ Arrange apple slices on greens.
Sprinkle with crumbled blue cheese
and pecan pieces.

❧ Serve with Honey Dressing.

❧ Serves I

HAM MAYONNAISE

I cup mayonnaise (preferably
  homemade)
½ cup finely ground ham
2 tablespoons finely chopped dill
  pickle
I teaspoon prepared mustard

❧ Mix mayonnaise, ham, pickle, and
mustard. Store in covered container
in refrigerator.

❧ Makes I ½ cups

HONEY DRESSING

⅔ cup sugar
I teaspoon dry mustard
I teaspoon paprika
¼ teaspoon salt
I teaspoon poppy seeds
I teaspoon grated onion
⅓ cup honey
5 tablespoons vinegar
I tablespoon lemon juice
I cup vegetable oil

❧ Place sugar, mustard, paprika, salt,
and poppy seeds in food processor.
Pulse on-off to blend.

❧ Add onion, honey, vinegar, and
lemon juice, and blend. While processor is running, slowly add oil.
Store in jar in refrigerator.

❧ Makes 2 cups

BOILED DRESSING FOR POTATO OR CHICKEN SALAD
A sweet-and-sour dressing

2 eggs
⅓ cup vinegar
3 tablespoons sugar
Salt and pepper to taste
I cup mayonnaise
I tablespoon celery seeds
¼ cup minced onion
I cup chopped celery

❧ Beat eggs and add vinegar, sugar,
salt, and pepper. Cook in small
saucepan over medium heat until
thickened, stirring constantly. Mix
with mayonnaise, celery seed, and
onion. Add celery and dressing to
potato or chicken salad when dressing has cooled.

❧ Makes 2 cups

SWEET RELISH MARINADE

I teaspoon salt
⅛ teaspoon freshly ground black
  pepper
¼ teaspoon paprika
Few grains cayenne
½ cup olive oil
3 tablespoons wine vinegar
½ tablespoon chopped parsley
½ tablespoon chopped chives
I tablespoon grated onion
I tablespoon chopped pimiento
I tablespoon sweet pickle relish

❧ Combine salt, pepper, paprika,
and cayenne in blender. Slowly add
oil and vinegar alternately to form
an emulsion. Add parsley, chives,
onion, pimiento, and pickle relish.
Chill in covered jar 2 to 3 hours
until flavors blend.

❧ Serving suggestions: Pour over a
combination of sliced mushrooms,
sliced celery, and sliced green onions
and serve on Bibb lettuce. Also good
as a marinade for asparagus or green
beans.

❧ Makes approximately I cup

BREAD

PLUM KUCHEN

1 ½ cups flour
2 teaspoons baking powder
½ teaspoon salt
1 cup sugar, divided
½ cup vegetable shortening
1 egg, beaten
½ cup milk
18 Italian blue plums, pitted and
    quartered
½ teaspoon cinnamon
3 tablespoons butter, melted

⚅ Preheat oven to 375°. Grease 13 x 9 x 2-inch pan.

⚅ Sift flour, baking powder, salt, and ½ cup sugar into large bowl. Cut in the shortening with a pastry blender until crumbly. Stir in the egg and milk until mixture is moist. Spread evenly in the greased baking pan. Arrange the plums in rows on top.

⚅ Mix the remaining ½ cup sugar and cinnamon in a cup and sprinkle over the plums. Drizzle with the melted butter.

⚅ Bake for 30 minutes, or until golden and a toothpick inserted in the center comes out clean. Bake at 350° if using a glass pan. Serve warm.

⚅ Serves 12

LOOKAWAY FARM BREAD
*Easy, delicious, and satisfying —
no sugar, no fat*

1 package dry yeast
2 ¼ cups warm water (110° to 115°), divided
5 ¾ cups unbleached flour, divided
1 teaspoon salt

⚅ Dissolve yeast in ¼ cup warm water in large bowl. Stir in ¾ cup flour until it forms a ball. Remove from bowl. Put 2 cups warm water in same bowl with salt. Put dough ball into warm water 15 to 20 minutes. Dump 5 cups flour in at once. Stir until well combined.

⚅ Knead on floured board 10 minutes. Let rise in bowl until doubled in bulk. Divide into 2 equal parts and allow to rest 10 minutes.

⚅ Place in 2 buttered loaf pans and let rise until doubled in bulk.

⚅ Preheat oven to 400°.

⚅ Bake loaves for 15 minutes. Turn down heat to 350° and bake an additional 30 minutes. Cool on racks. May be frozen well wrapped.

⚅ Makes 2 loaves

"RIZE" ROLLS
An old family biscuit recipe

1 ¼-ounce package dry yeast
1 cup buttermilk
2 tablespoons sugar
½ teaspoon baking soda
2 ½ cups self-rising flour
    (plus a small amount
    for handling dough)
½ cup shortening
¼ cup butter, melted

⚅ Dissolve yeast in warm (110° to 115°) buttermilk.

⚅ Place sugar, baking soda, and flour in bowl of food processor with steel blade. Pulse on-off to blend. Add shortening and pulse until dry ingredients are like fine cornmeal.

⚅ While processor is running, add yeast mixture and process until mixture forms a ball. Remove and knead a few times on floured board.

⚅ Roll dough out thinly, brush with melted butter, fold dough over, roll out, and brush with butter again..

⚅ Cut with 2-inch cutter, place on baking sheet and let rise 1 hour. Bake at 400° 10 to 12 minutes.

⚅ Makes 3 dozen

HUSH PUPPIES
A must with any fried fish

1 pound (about 3 ½ cups)
    cornmeal
1 teaspoon salt
⅛ teaspoon soda
3 tablespoons sugar (optional)
½ cup finely chopped onion
1 egg, beaten
1 cup buttermilk
1 ⅓ cups water
Oil for frying

⚅ Stir together cornmeal, salt, soda, and sugar, if desired. Add onion and blend. Mix beaten egg and buttermilk. Add to dry ingredients. Carefully stir in water and thoroughly blend.

⚅ In deep skillet or heavy pan, heat oil to 375°. Using 2 tablespoons, form into golf-ball-size portions and drop mixture into hot oil and fry until evenly browned. Drain on paper towels. Serve hot.

⚅ Serves 6 to 8

DESSERTS

MINT SHERBET
*No dessert is
cooler or more refreshing.*

2 cups sugar
2 cups water
1 cup packed, chopped fresh mint
    leaves
Juice of 2 lemons
1 cup orange juice
Green food coloring

❆ Bring sugar and water to boil and
remove from heat. Add mint leaves
and lemon juice. Let stand 1 hour,
crushing and mashing leaves to
extract flavor. Strain. Add orange
juice and tint with food coloring.

❆ Freeze in 8 x 8-inch pan until
mushy. Stir well with fork and continue freezing until firm.

❆ Serves 4

SPRING CREAM WITH BERRIES
*Keep a bagful in the freezer for a
quick, elegant dessert.*

1 8-ounce package cream cheese
1 cup confectioners' sugar
1 cup light cream
½ teaspoon vanilla
Berries, whole or mashed

❆ Soften cream cheese. Beat with
mixer until smooth. Beat in sugar.
Add cream and vanilla.

❆ Pour into fluted paper liners in
muffin pans. Freeze.

❆ When frozen, they may be
removed from pans and put in freezer bags until ready to use. Peel off
paper before serving.

❆ May be bedded on sliced, sweetened berries, on raspberry purée, or
with any berries spooned over.

❆ Serves 8

TIGER LILY CAKE
An alternative to fruit cake

3 cups sugar, divided
6 eggs
1 ½ cups butter
    (no substitutions)
4 cups flour, divided
2 teaspoons baking powder
2 teaspoons cloves
2 teaspoons allspice
2 teaspoons cinnamon
2 teaspoons nutmeg
1 teaspoon salt
1 cup milk
2 15-ounce boxes golden raisins
2 pounds pecan halves
Bourbon whiskey

❆ Preheat oven to 300°.

❆ Beat 1 ½ cups sugar with eggs.

❆ In large bowl, cream butter and
1 ½ cups sugar. Add to egg mixture.

❆ Sift 3 cups flour, baking powder,
cloves, allspice, cinnamon, nutmeg,
and salt. Add alternately with milk,
mixing well.

❆ Toss raisins and nuts in 1 cup
flour. Add to batter.

❆ Line 1 large tube pan with foil.
Fill with batter and bake at 300° 3
½ hours or until tested done. When
removed from oven, wait 5 minutes,
then liberally pour bourbon whiskey
over cake. Allow to cool.

❆ Remove from pan and wrap tightly. Refrigerate at least 1 day before
slicing.

❆ May be frozen. When thawed,
add more bourbon.

❆ Makes 1 5-pound cake, 40 to 50
servings

APPLE SUPREME

½ stick unsalted butter or margarine
¼ cup brown sugar
½ cup brandy
1 tablespoon fresh lemon juice
2 ¼ teaspoons cinnamon, divided
   or to taste
4 tart cooking apples, peeled,
   cored, and sliced into
   ¼-inch pieces
1 quart vanilla ice cream

✳ Melt butter in large skillet. Stir in
brown sugar, brandy, lemon juice,
and ¼ teaspoon cinnamon.

✳ Add apples and stir to coat well.
Cover and cook on low heat, stirring
often, until apples are tender.

✳ Soften ice cream in bowl and
quickly stir in 2 teaspoons cinnamon. Refreeze.

✳ At serving time, warm apples and
spoon over ice cream.

✳ Serves 6

LUCY'S DAMSON PLUM PIE

3 eggs
1 cup sugar
½ cup melted butter
1 cup damson plum preserves
   with peel
2 unbaked pie crusts

✳ Preheat oven to 375°.

✳ Beat eggs until very light. Stir in
sugar, butter, and preserves until just
mixed.

✳ Pour into pie crusts and bake until
firm in center, about 25 minutes.
Cool and serve.

✳ Makes 2 pies

CHRISTMAS CAKE
*Makes a pretty presentation and a
change from usual holiday cakes*

4 eggs
1 cup plus 2 to 3 tablespoons
   sugar, divided
½ cup flour
1 teaspoon baking powder
2 teaspoons vanilla
1 cup chopped dates
1 cup chopped pecans
2 cups mandarin oranges
2 to 3 bananas
1 pint cream, whipped
1 tablespoon brandy or
   Grand Marnier liqueur
1 can shredded coconut
1 maraschino cherry

✳ Preheat oven to 350°.

✳ Beat eggs until light and add 1
cup sugar, stirring to blend.

✳ Sift flour and baking powder. Add
to egg mixture along with vanilla,
dates, and pecans. Pour into greased
8 x 8-inch cake pan.

✳ Bake 30 to 35 minutes. Cool on
rack.

✳ Drain oranges. Slice and sprinkle
bananas with 2 to 3 tablespoons
sugar.

✳ To assemble, break up cake and
outline a 9-inch-diameter circle on
serving plate with pieces of cake.
Layer fruit and cake pieces to make a
pyramid.

✳ Frost cake with whipped cream,
sprinkle with coconut, and top with
cherry. Chill until serving time.

✳ Serves 8

THE COUNCIL OF THE VIRGINIA MUSEUM OF FINE ARTS COOKBOOK COMMITTEE

Chairman:
Ruth Cunningham

Co-chairman:
Dorothy Boehm

Computer Production:
Fran Johns

Recipe Chairman:
Xan Rogers

Recipe Committee:
Jane Bundy
Liz Cone
Ginger Levit
Bryant Pilcher
Rogie Williams

Recipe Coordinator:
Elsie Palmore

Testing Chairman:
Sue Crowell

Area Chairmen:
Win Crosgrove
Frances Park
Frances Schools
Mary Speight
Nancy Thomas
Doris Trainer

Photography Props:
Telia Blackard

Treasurer:
Jackie Spiers

Special Advisor:
Elsie Donahoe

Marketing Chairman:
Anne Brasfield

Marketing Committee:
Carol Adelaar
Sara Allen
Graham Basto
Betty Bauder
Dian Bergner
Joanne Carron
Kitten Clarke
B. J. Durrill
Sally Flinn
Peg Freeman
Norma Jean Joyner
Anne Miller
Charlotte Minor
Pam Reynolds
Carol Ann Ross
Weasie Stuart
Barbara Thalhimer

Office Manager:
Michael Robertson

Newsletter:
Glad Applegate

RECIPE CONTRIBUTORS

Sara Allen
Billy Allen
Campbell Argenzio
Millie Arnette
Ann Artz
Candi Baird
Katherine Barrett
Carol Battista
Dian Bergner
Audrey Black
Mary Rives Black
Demie Blair
Shep Blair
Jackson Blanton
Lucy Blanton
Margarette Blundon
Dorothy Boehm
Carolyn Bowman
Betsy Bredrup
Polly Brooks
Emma Brown
Carol Bruehl
Eddie Brush
Jane Bundy
Joanne Carron
Ann Cecil
Jane Scott Chapin
Kay Chapman
Millie Chevalier
Kitty Claiborne
Mary Lou Clarke
Kitten Clarke
Louise Cochrane
Pat Coffield
Liz Cone
Caroline Cooke
Win Cosgrove
True Coxe
Doris Crickenberger
Charlotte Cridlin
Sue Crowell
Marguerite Crumley
Ruth Crumley
Ruth Cunningham
Elisabeth Dawes
Sally Dawson
Mary Dombalis
Frances Duke
Sue Duncan
Victoria Lee Edwards
Barbara Ellington
Nancy Elliott
Sally Erickson
Mikki Evens
Patty Fairlamb
Jo Ann Fallon
Bonnie Farmer
Sally Flinn
Clare Fonville

Jean Frederick
Peg Freeman
Mallory Freeman
Ruth Fuleihan
Katherine Gill
Judy Gilman
Josette Gleason
Sissy Gorsline
Liza Graham
Josette Gleason
Jean Gregg
Ann Grimsley
Conny Hancock
Carolyn Harbison
Carey Harding
Ruth Harp
Gail Harris
Jeanne Harris
Christopher Harrison
Sarah Harrison
Mary Harwood
Evelyn Helwig
Dallas Henderson
Inez Henry
Knight Hill
Lyn Hodnett
Catherine Hoke
Kitty Holt
Madeline Hutton
Anne Jackson
Marriott Jackson
Mary Moore Jacoby
Patricia Jagoda
Helen Scott Jenkins
Anne Jennings
Jane Joel
Barbara Jones
Mary Jo Kearfott
Jan Kennedy
Cindy Kloeti
Betty Koonce
Suegenia Kympton
Frances Lambert
Rosemary Lanahan
Dovie Lee
Ginger Levit
Joyce Lovelace
Bobbie Lublin
Ginny MacIvor
Phyllis Macilroy
Virginia Maloney
Elise Maloy
Mary Leigh Marston
Emma Lou Martin
Bess Martine
Shirlee Maxson
Sonia McDonald
Virginia McDonough
Janet McGee
Caroline McGehee
Mary Melton

Mary Merrell
Nan Meyer
Loretta Miller
Fran Miner
Doug Moncure
Sarah Lee Moncure
Betsy Gates Moore
Martha Morrill
Nancy Morris
Nancy Morrissette
Janet Murphree
Vivian Murphy
Maureen Neal
Jean Nichols
Barbara O'Flaherty
Margaret Page
Elsie Palmore
Fran Park
Ruth Perel
Joanne Perrot
Patsy Pettus
Ora Lee Pitts
Beth Powell
Hermie Powell
Lou Preston
Doris Radcliff
Jane Reid
M. S. Rennick
Inger Rice
Margaret Robbins
Xan Rogers
Mary Kaye Rose
Mimi Rose
Joyce Rosenbaum
Sam Rosenthal
Ellen Rueger
Mary Anne Sartin
Frances Schools
Hilda Schroetter
Jean Shields
Bette Shiflett
Sandy Smollich
Eleanor Smart
Mary Estes Speight
Betty Stinson
Virginia Strang
Ann Strange
Anne Suddeth
Naomi Taylor
Martha Thomas
Nancy Thomas
Gloria Thompson
Jessie Thompson
Beth Thornton
Doris Trainer
Cathy Tullidge
Payne Tyler
Mary Martin Ullman
Nancy Vaughan
Jean Vertner

Virginia Museum
  Dining Room
Charline Watkins
Nancy Weisiger
Mary Elliott Wheeler
Martha White
Luisa Whiting
Lillian Whitney
Miriam Wickham
Nancy Williams
Rogie Williams
Sally Williams
Susan Wilson
Dudley Wiltshire
Connie Wirth
Isabel Witt
Cathy Yancey

COOKBOOK TESTERS

Billy Allen
Margaret Austin
Shep Blair
Betsy Bredrup
Emma Brown
Carol Bruehl
Joanne Carron
Liz Cone
True Coxe
Charlotte Cridlin
Marguerite Crumley
Ruth Crumley
Sally Dawson
Vicky Edwards
Sally Erickson
Bonnie Farmer
Judy Gilman
Liza Graham
Gail Harris
Jean Hart
Minnie Held
Dallas Henderson
Lyn Hodnett
Cathy Hoke
Ann Jennings
Fran Johns
Hariet Kent
Suegenia Kympton
Nancy Leary
Dovie Lee
Ginger Levit
Bobby Lublin
Ginny MacIvor
Virginia Maloney
Janet Murphree
Margaret Page
Fran Park
Joanne Perrot
Margaret Robbins
Xan Rogers
Mary Kaye Rose

Hilda Schroetter
Ann Strange
Marti Thomas
Gloria Thompson
Jessie Thompson
Cathy Tullidge
Mary Martin Ullman
Nancy Williams
Sally Williams
Isabella Witt

ACKNOWLEDGE-MENTS

Michael Coleman Adam
Henry Anderson
Robert Blair Antiques
Sam Barnes
Compleat Gourmet, Inc.
Bill Ellis
Four Seasons Fan Flowers
Mr. and Mrs. Edwin B.
  Gregg
Mr. and Mrs. Bruce
  Gottwald
Hampton House –
  E. B. Taylor
Mary Jones Helm
J. Taylor Hogan, Inc.
Keith Knost
Kitchen Kuisine
Mr. and Mrs. Jack
  Lanahan
Mr. and Mrs. Ralph H.
  Lovelace
Mrs. Julia Martine
Mr. and Mrs. William E.
  Massey, Jr.
William G. McClure III
Elizabeth P. Miller
The Mixing Bowl
Paper Plus
Dr. Herbert Park
Mr. and Mrs. Coleman
  Perrin
Dr. and Mrs. Watson O.
  Powell, Jr.
David F. Sidoti
Nancy Smith
Stedman House
Marti Thomas
Tuckahoe Plantation
Virginia Museum
  Gift Shop
Wicker in the Wind
Kay Williams
Mr. and Mrs. Coleman
  Wortham
WRVA
Staff of The Virginia
  Museum of Fine Arts

INDEX